NURSING

FOURTH EDITION

Ferguson's
An Infobase Learning Company

Careers in Focus: Nursing

Copyright © 2011 by Infobase Learning

Ferguson's
An imprint of Infobase Learning
132 West 31st Street
New York NY 10001

Library of Congress Cataloging-in-Publication Data

Careers in focus. Nursing. — 4th ed.
    p. cm. — (Careers in focus)
    Includes bibliographical references and index.
    ISBN-13: 978-0-8160-8034-2 (hardcover : alk. paper)
    ISBN-10: 0-8160-8034-8 (hardcover : alk. paper)   1. Nursing—Juvenile literature.   2. Nursing—Vocational guidance—Juvenile literature.   I. Ferguson Publishing.   II. Title: Nursing.
    RT61.5.C374 2010
    610.73023—dc22

                                                            2010049443

Ferguson's books are available at special discounts when purchased in bulk quantities for businesses, associations, institutions, or sales promotions. Please call our Special Sales Department in New York at (212) 967-8800 or (800) 322-8755.

You can find Ferguson's on the World Wide Web at
http://www.infobaselearning.com

Text design by David Strelecky
Composition by Newgen
Cover printed by Yurchak Printing, Landisville, PA
Book printed and bound by Yurchak Printing, Landisville, PA
Date printed: May 2011
Printed in the United States of America

10 9 8 7 6 5 4 3 2 1

This book is printed on acid-free paper.

All links and Web addresses were checked and verified to be correct at the time of publication. Because of the dynamic nature of the Web, some addresses and links may have changed since publication and may no longer be valid.

Table of Contents

Introduction

Nursing is an exciting, yet demanding, career field that offers a variety of diverse career paths and employment settings. Registered nurses, in particular, may work in many settings besides hospitals. For example, *occupational health nurses* oversee the health needs of business and government employees in their workplaces. *Public health nurses* specialize in promoting good health practices to prevent illness and restore health; they may provide care and counseling in schools, clinics, or other settings. *Office nurses* generally assist physicians, surgeons, and sometimes dentists in private practice or in clinics, often performing routine office and laboratory work in addition to nursing services. Other registered nurses teach, staff nursing organizations, act as administrators, or work as part of a legal team.

Advanced practice nurses are a broad category of registered nurses who have completed advanced clinical nurses' educational practice requirements beyond the two to four years of basic nursing education required for all RNs. Under the advanced practice nursing designation fall four categories of nursing specialties: *clinical nurse specialists, nurse practitioners, nurse-midwives,* and *nurse anesthetists.* Advanced practice nurses embody the expanding and increasingly powerful role of nurses in health care. In particular, nurse practitioners and *physician assistants* are becoming key personnel in many medical practices, as they provide many of the same types of basic care as a physician would, but at a reduced cost. They also enable medical practices to treat a larger patient base.

The strong demand for nurses is not limited to the United States. There is a need for nurses all over the world, especially in developing countries struggling with overpopulation, malnutrition, infectious diseases, and a lack of medical facilities. Nurses who choose to work in rural areas of developing countries usually do not have the equipment and medicine available in the United States. Thus, a large part of their work is education—teaching basic health and wellness principles to the general population and training local people to be nurses. Such international opportunities are often temporary and done on a volunteer basis. These opportunities exist in the United States, as well. Entry-level nurses or nurses who are re-entering the workforce can volunteer to gain additional career experience.

There is no denying that nursing is a challenging and stressful career. It is physically demanding, requiring strength, stamina, and speed. It is emotionally draining, particularly for those who work with chronically ill and dying patients. Nursing demands a ready knowledge of medical techniques and procedures, keen observation skills, and meticulous attention to detail. Nurses must be able to communicate effectively with patients, physicians, administrators, and patients' families. Nurses' work is often taken for granted. Because of these pressures, there is significant burnout in the nursing professions.

Even though those who go into nursing soon learn about these pressures, most nurses say that the rewards of their careers are far greater than any drawbacks. Nurses are caring, nurturing individuals. They get great satisfaction from caring for sick or injured patients, guiding them through the healing process, and watching them respond to treatment. Nurses who care for terminally ill patients find accomplishment in knowing that they are providing comfort and relief from physical and emotional pain. Nurses are a vital link between patients and other medical professionals, and they often act as patient advocates and spokespersons. Simply put, the health care industry could not exist without nurses.

Although nursing has typically been a profession for Caucasian women, that profile is rapidly changing. Today, men and women of all ages, ethnicities, and socioeconomic backgrounds choose careers in nursing. Many come to the field after working in other areas of health care or in other industries, which has resulted in a richer, more diversified nursing workforce than ever before.

Because of the rapidly growing U.S. elderly population and continued advances in medical technology, the U.S. Department of Labor projects that employment for registered nurses will grow much faster than the average for all careers through 2018. Opportunities will be especially strong for those with advanced education and a willingness to work in underserved areas such as inner cities or rural areas.

Each article in *Careers in Focus: Nursing* discusses a particular nursing occupation in detail. The articles appear in Ferguson's *Encyclopedia of Careers and Vocational Guidance*, but they have been updated and revised with the latest information from the U.S. Department of Labor, professional organizations, and other sources. In addition, this revised edition of the book includes a new article on *forensic nurses*.

Since many advanced nursing careers, such as clinical nurse specialists, *nurse managers*, and nurse-midwives, require that the individual first become a registered nurse, it is recommended that you read the article "Registered Nurses" first, as it discusses in detail the educational requirements and other specifics of that career.

The **Quick Facts** section provides a brief summary of the career, including recommended school subjects, personal skills, work environment, minimum educational requirements, salary ranges, certification or licensing requirements, and employment outlook. This section also provides acronyms and identification numbers for the following government classification indexes: the Dictionary of Occupational Titles (DOT), the Guide for Occupational Exploration (GOE), the National Occupational Classification (NOC) Index, and the Occupational Information Network (O*NET)-Standard Occupational Classification System (SOC) index. The DOT, GOE, and O*NET-SOC indexes have been created by the U.S. government; the NOC index is Canada's career classification system. Readers can use the identification numbers listed in the Quick Facts section to access further information about a career. Print editions of the DOT (*Dictionary of Occupational Titles*. Indianapolis, Ind.: JIST Works, 1991) and GOE (*Guide for Occupational Exploration*. Indianapolis, Ind.: JIST Works, 2001) are available at libraries. Electronic versions of the DOT (http://www.oalj.dol.gov/libdot.htm), NOC (http://www5.hrsdc.gc.ca/NOC), and O*NET-SOC (http://online.onetcenter.org) are available on the Internet. When no DOT, GOE, NOC, or O*NET-SOC numbers are listed, this means that the U.S. Department of Labor or Human Resources and Skills Development Canada have not created a numerical designation for this career. In this instance, you will see the acronym "N/A," or not available.

The **Overview** section is a brief introductory description of the duties and responsibilities involved in this career. Oftentimes, a career may have a variety of job titles. When this is the case, alternative career titles are presented. Employment statistics are also provided, when available. The **History** section describes the history of the particular job as it relates to the overall development of its industry or field. **The Job** describes the primary and secondary duties of the job. **Requirements** discusses high school and postsecondary education and training requirements, any certification or licensing that is necessary, and other personal requirements for success in the job. **Exploring** offers suggestions on how to gain experience in or knowledge of the particular job before making a firm educational and financial commitment. The focus is on what can be done while still in high school (or in the early years of college) to gain a better understanding of the job. The **Employers** section gives an overview of typical places of employment for the job. **Starting Out** discusses the best ways to land that first job, be it through the college career services office, newspaper ads, Internet employment sites, or personal contact. The **Advancement** section describes what kind of career path to expect from the job and how to get there. **Earnings** lists salary ranges and describes the typical fringe benefits. The **Work Environment** section describes the typical surroundings and conditions of employment—whether indoors or outdoors, noisy or quiet, social or independent. Also discussed are typical hours worked, any seasonal fluctuations, and the stresses and strains of the job. The **Outlook** section summarizes the job in terms of the general economy and industry projections. For the most part, Outlook information is obtained from the U.S. Bureau of Labor Statistics and is supplemented by information gathered from professional associations. Job growth terms follow those used in the *Occupational Outlook Handbook*. Growth described as "much faster than the average" means an increase of 20 percent or more. Growth described as "faster than the average" means an increase of 14 to 19 percent. Growth described as "about as fast as the average" means an increase of 7 to 13 percent. Growth described as "more slowly than the average" means an increase of 3 to 6 percent. "Little or no change" means a decrease of 2 percent to an increase of 2 percent. "Decline" means a decrease of 3 percent or more. Each article ends with **For More Information**, which lists organizations that provide information on training, education, internships, scholarships, and job placement.

Careers in Focus: Nursing also includes photos, informative sidebars, and interviews with professionals in the field.

Clinical Nurse Specialists

OVERVIEW

Clinical nurse specialists (CNSs), a classification of *advanced practice nurses*, are registered nurses who have completed advanced clinical nurses' educational practice requirements. Qualified to handle a wide variety of physical and mental health problems, CNSs are primarily involved in providing primary health care and psychotherapy. Approximately 99,400 clinical nurse specialists are employed in the United States.

HISTORY

The National League for Nursing Education first drew up a plan to create the clinical nurse specialist role in the 1940s. The first master's degree program opened in 1954 at Rutgers University; the only specialty offered at that time was psychiatric nursing. By 1970, clinical nurse specialty certification had become available in a number of fields in response to the increased specialization in health care, the development of new technologies, and the need to provide alternative, cost-efficient health care in the physician shortage of the 1960s.

THE JOB

Clinical nurse specialists conduct health assessments and evaluations based on the patient's history, laboratory tests, and their own personal examinations. Following such assessments they arrive at a diagnosis of the patient's problem and deliver care and develop

Learn More About It

Catalano, Joseph T. *Nursing Now: Today's Issues, Tomorrow's Trends.* 5th ed. Philadelphia: F. A. Davis Company, 2008.

Novotny, Jeanne M., Doris T. Lippman, Nicole K. Sanders, and Joyce J. Fitzpatrick. *101 Careers in Nursing.* New York: Springer Publishing Company, 2006.

Peterson, Veronica. *Just the Facts: A Pocket Guide to Nursing.* 4th ed. St. Louis: Mosby, 2008.

Potter, Patricia A., and Anne Griffin Perry. *Fundamentals of Nursing.* 7th ed. St. Louis: Mosby, 2009.

Smith, Sandra F., Donna Duell, and Barbara Martin. *Clinical Nursing Skills: Basic to Advanced.* 7th ed. Upper Saddle River, N.J.: Prentice Hall, 2007.

Vallano, Annette. *Your Career In Nursing: Manage Your Future in the Changing World of Healthcare.* 5th ed. New York: Kaplan Publishing, 2008.

quality-control methods to help correct the patient's medical problem. In addition to delivering direct patient care, clinical nurse specialists may be involved in consultation, research, education, and administration. They may specialize in one or more areas, such as pediatrics, mental health, perinatal care, oncology, or gerontology. A few work independently or in private practice and are qualified for reimbursement by Medicare, Medicaid, and other federally sponsored or private health care payers.

REQUIREMENTS

High School

If you are interested in pursuing a career in nursing, you should take college-preparatory courses in chemistry, health, biology, human anatomy, computer science, and mathematics. Speech and English classes that help you develop your communication skills (both oral and written) are also important.

Postsecondary Training

If you want to become a clinical nurse specialist, you will first need to complete the high school and undergraduate education necessary to become a registered nurse. (See "Registered Nurses.")

CNSs must earn a master's or higher degree after completing their studies to become a registered nurse. Many CNSs go on to earn their doctoral degrees. CNSs can specialize by focusing their studies in a specific area, such as community health, home health, gerontology, or medical-surgical. The National Association of Clinical Nurse Specialists provides a list of educational programs at its Web site, http://www.nacns.org.

Certification or Licensing

CNS certification is available through the American Nurses Credentialing Center. Applicants must have completed education and experience requirements before taking the certification test. Certification is available in nearly 10 subspecialties. Other certifications are offered by the Oncology Nursing Certification Corporation, the American Association of Critical Care Nurses Certification Corporation, and the Orthopaedic Nurses Certification Board.

All states and the District of Columbia require a license to practice nursing. To obtain a license, graduates of approved nursing schools must pass a national examination. Nurses may be licensed by more than one state. In some states, continuing education is a condition for license renewal.

Other Requirements

Anyone going into nursing needs to have a caring attitude and a strong commitment to helping people. Emotional maturity, a well-balanced personality, and excellent communication skills are vital.

In addition to possessing the qualities shared by all good nurses, clinical nurse specialists need to develop the leadership skills and expert competence necessary for advanced practice nursing. Because the clinical nurse specialist role is still not understood by some doctors and nurses, he or she must have the professional self-confidence to educate colleagues as well as patients and families. Physicians may be reluctant to recognize the qualifications of the clinical nurse specialist, and staff nurses may be resistant to what they perceive as criticism or interference with their work. A clinical nurse specialist also needs to have the academic interest and ability to do graduate study. A master's degree is required, and a doctorate is becoming increasingly necessary for top-level positions involving research, teaching, and policy making.

EXPLORING

You can explore your interest in the nursing field in a number of ways. You can visit nursing-oriented Web sites and talk with high school counselors, school nurses, and local public health nurses. Visit hospitals to observe the work and to talk with hospital personnel.

Reading books about nursing and the clinical nurse specialty will also be helpful. Here is one suggestion: *The Clinical Nurse Specialist Handbook*, 2nd edition, by Patti Rager Zuzelo (Sudbury, Mass.: Jones & Bartlett Publishers, 2009).

EMPLOYERS

More than 99,400 clinical nurse specialists are employed in the United States. Clinical nurse specialists work in a wide range of health care settings, depending on their particular area of specialization and interest. They are employed in hospitals, clinics, community health centers, mental health facilities, nursing homes, home health care agencies, veterans affairs facilities, nursing schools and other educational institutions, physicians' offices, and the military. A few are in private or independent practice.

STARTING OUT

Information about job openings for clinical nurse specialists is available from many sources. Your nursing school career services office is the best place to start; other avenues include nursing registries, nurse employment agencies, and state employment offices. Positions are often listed in professional journals and newspapers. Information about government jobs is available from the Office of Personnel Management for your region. Contacts you have made through clinical work or involvement in professional societies can be helpful sources of information. The organization that formerly employed you as a staff nurse may be eager to rehire you as a clinical nurse specialist once you have received your master's degree in nursing and been certified in an advanced practice specialty. Additionally, the National Association of Clinical Nurse Specialists provides job listings at its Web site, http://www.nacns.org.

ADVANCEMENT

As clinical nurse specialists gain experience, they become qualified for positions that involve greater responsibility and give them opportunities to have a greater impact on nursing practice. Some people choose to broaden their base of expertise by adding nurse practitioner qualifications to their credentials.

Many clinical nurse specialists become involved in nursing education, research, publishing, and consulting. Some may want to make their voices heard in the current debate on the future of health care.

Moving into faculty or administrative positions is the form of advancement chosen by some clinical nurse specialists, while others prefer to remain in positions that are more direct-care oriented.

EARNINGS

According to Salary.com, the nationwide median salary for CNSs in November 2010 was $86,084. Salaries ranged from less than $71,627 to $100,542 or more. The National Association of Clinical Nurse Specialists reports that very experienced clinical nurse specialists can earn more than $110,000 annually. The U.S. Bureau of Labor Statistics reports that salaries for medical and health services managers, a category that includes CNSs, ranged from less than $49,750 to more than $140,300, with a median of $81,850, in 2009.

Benefits for full-time workers include paid vacation, health, disability, and life insurance, and retirement or pension plans.

WORK ENVIRONMENT

CNSs work primarily in hospitals, clinics, or nursing homes but may work out of their own homes and other community-based settings, including industry, home health care, and health maintenance organizations.

OUTLOOK

Clinical nurse specialists are in high demand due to their blend of administrative knowledge and patient-centered care. Thus, advanced practice nurses with the proper credentials and certification should have no trouble finding posts in a wide variety of health care facilities in the next decade. Opportunities will be strongest in inner cities and rural areas.

FOR MORE INFORMATION

For information on certification, contact
American Nurses Credentialing Center
8515 Georgia Avenue, Suite 400
Silver Spring, MD 20910-3492
Tel: 800-284-2378
http://www.nursecredentialing.org

For additional information on education, training, and career opportunities, contact

National Association of Clinical Nurse Specialists
100 North 20th Street, 4th Floor
Philadelphia, PA 19103-1462
Tel: 215-320-3881
http://www.nacns.org

INTERVIEW

Garrett K. Chan, RN, PhD, CNS, FPCN, FAEN, is a clinical nurse specialist in the Emergency Department Observation Unit as well as the Palliative Care Service at Stanford Hospital & Clinics, a Level I Trauma Center in California. He is also an associate clinical professor in the Department of Physiological Nursing at the University of California, San Francisco. Garrett discussed his career with the editors of Careers in Focus: Nursing.

Q. How long have you worked in the field? What made you want to enter this career?

A. I graduated from my pre-licensure nursing program in 1996 and began working in an emergency department (ED) the following year. I found being a staff nurse very rewarding and I wanted to learn more about the management of complex and vulnerable patient populations. That was what drew me to the clinical nurse specialist (CNS) role. In 1998, the CNS role was recognized as having an advanced practice that included five sub-roles: expert clinician, educator, change agent, researcher, and consultant. By learning new skills at the graduate level in these five sub-roles, I would be able to effect change in many arenas in health care—at the bedside, within health care organizations, in public health, and in health policy.

   I entered the University of California, San Francisco Critical Care/Trauma Clinical Nurse Specialist program in 1998. This program provided an outstanding foundation to diagnose and treat illness, provide expert consultation in difficult situations, manage change within and across health care systems, collaborate with other members of multidisciplinary teams to optimize clinical outcomes, provide skillful guidance to interdisciplinary teams, and evaluate research and its applicability to practice. These activities are also the core competencies for clinical nurse specialists as delineated by the National Association of Clinical Nurse Specialists.

Q. **Can you please briefly describe a day in your life on the job as a clinical nurse specialist?**

A. Clinical nurse specialist activities fall in three substantive areas of practice: manage the care of complex and vulnerable populations; educate and support interdisciplinary staff; and facilitate change and innovation within health care systems. These activities differentiate the clinical nurse specialist from the other three advanced practice nurse roles of nurse practitioner, nurse-midwife, and nurse anesthetist.

Every day, I round in the Emergency Department Observation Unit. I look for the patients who might have complex conditions or who may be particularly vulnerable due to their physiological, psychological, or social issues. I collaborate with the nurses, nurse practitioner or physician assistant, and emergency attending physician regarding the plan of care of the patients and possibly recommend treatment or diagnostic testing. I also do some education for the team based on my recommendations.

After my morning rounds, I then start working on projects that will improve the care delivery to patients and families. One current project I am working on is creating an order set for diagnosing, observation, and treatment for transient ischemic attacks (TIAs). TIAs are transient (i.e., resolving) focal neurological deficits like arm weakness or inability to speak that are similar to strokes. These patients are at higher risk for developing a stroke. So, I work with Emergency Medicine, Neurology, and Radiology [departments] to design system processes to either rule in or rule out stroke, TIA, or other medical conditions in a timely manner. I work with Nursing to ensure that appropriate neurological checks are completed to quickly identify any deterioration in condition. Additionally, I critique and evaluate the literature to ensure that the interventions and outcomes are based in the evidence.

Q. **What are some of the pros and cons of your job?**

A. The benefits of the CNS role include focusing on complex patients and families, educating interdisciplinary staff, creating innovative programs to improve nursing and health care, and flexibility of the schedule. Although not present in my current job, cons of being a clinical nurse specialist may include the misunderstanding of this role among others in the health care field and the public that can lead to the misuse of CNSs. Examples of misuse of clinical nurse specialists can include having the CNS focus solely on providing nursing education, leading quality/process improvement activities, and being responsible for all regulatory compliance. The clinical nurse specialist must maintain a direct clinical practice with the complex and vulnerable patient populations to ensure clinical competence. Additionally, understanding how the multidisciplinary staff functions in the ED will ensure that I make system change recommendations that are supportive and not too onerous.

Q. What are the most important personal and professional qualities for clinical nurse specialists?

A. Personal and professional qualities of a successful CNS include a sense of innovation, ability to process complex information, good interpersonal skills, leadership qualities, self-direction, and ability to inspire and encourage others.

Q. What advice would you give to young people who are interested in the field?

A. Potential CNS students must complete a pre-licensure (RN) nursing program to become an RN They must also possess a bachelor's degree. Depending on the university that has the CNS program, the bachelor's degree may or may not need to be in nursing. After being in practice as a staff nurse, the CNS applicant should start looking for a CNS program. The National Association of Clinical Nurse Specialists (http://www.nacns .org) has a list of CNS programs throughout the United States. Ask to interview with the program director to find out about types of courses in the program, how many clinical hours are required, what types of clinical experiences are offered, and what substantive area of practice is covered in that program. Expertise of the program faculty should be present in your substantive area of practice of interest (e.g., emergency, acute care, maternal/child health, psychiatric nursing).

Q. What is the employment outlook for clinical nurse specialists?

A. The employment outlook for clinical nurse specialists is bright. Hospitals that seek Magnet® recognition through the American Nurses Credentialing Center are interested in hiring CNSs due to their expertise and educational background.

Graduates of CNS programs can function in a variety of positions within health care since their education is so comprehensive. CNS education includes coursework in advanced health assessment, pathophysiology, pharmacology, project management, research utilization and critique, and education. Given these sets of skills, CNSs can work in clinics with patient populations such as heart failure. In hospitals, clinical nurse specialists can be based in particular units or in service lines such as trauma, stroke, or palliative care. Not all institutions use the title of clinical nurse specialist. Therefore, I recommend reading the job descriptions of jobs that sound interesting to see if the role responsibilities and skill sets are consistent with CNS education and competency.

Community Health Nurses

QUICK FACTS

School Subjects
Biology
Chemistry

Personal Skills
Helping/teaching
Technical/scientific

Work Environment
Primarily indoors
Primarily multiple locations

Minimum Education Level
Some postsecondary training

Salary Range
$43,970 to $63,750 to
$93,700+

Certification or Licensing
Voluntary (certification)
Required by all states
(licensing)

Outlook
Much faster than the average

DOT
075

GOE
14.02.01

NOC
3152

O*NET-SOC
29-1111.00

OVERVIEW

Community health nurses, also known as *public health nurses*, provide community-based health care. They organize, promote, and deliver care to community groups in urban, rural, and remote settings. They may work in community health centers in large and small cities, or they may travel to remote locations to bring health care treatment and information to people living in those areas. They may provide public health services and educational programs to schools, correctional facilities, homeless shelters, elderly care facilities, and maternal and well-baby clinics. Some community health nurses provide specialized care in communities where immediate physician services are not available. Community health nurses often work for a state funded or federally funded agency, or a private health provider company.

HISTORY

Community health nursing in the United States began in the late 1800s when wealthy donors funded health education programs in poor communities. Government agencies also began funding health education and care programs that improved the lives of the poor or those who did not have access to health care. Lillian Wald is considered the first public health nurse. She cared for poor people in New York City and founded the Henry Street Settlement, a social service agency that is still in operation today.

The American Public Health Association was founded in 1872 to improve public health around the world. Community health nurses continue to play an important role in public health today—especially in poor and underserved areas.

THE JOB

Community health nurses work with many aspects of a community's population. Their duties vary greatly depending on their locale and assignments. Some community health nurses may instruct a class for expectant mothers, visit new parents to help them learn how to care for their new baby, talk with senior citizens about exercise and nutrition, or give immunizations at a community center or other site. Other community health nurses may travel to remote areas where health care is not readily available. Here they may work with a medical doctor or nurse practitioner to provide necessary medical care and health education. Community health nurses usually work with people of all ages, ranging in age from newborn to the elderly. They also may work with different groups of people, including immigrants, homeless shelter residents, and persons who are developmentally or physically challenged.

Community health nurses may also be educators who plan, promote, and administer community-wide wellness programs. They may also give presentations to area organizations, schools, and health care facilities regarding health, safety, exercise, and nutrition.

Nursing Resources on the Web

National Student Nurses' Association
http://www.nsna.org

Nurse.com
http://www.nurse.com

Nursing Fun
http://www.nursingfun.com

Nursing World
http://www.nursingworld.org

Yahoo!: Nursing
http://dir.yahoo.com/health/nursing

Some community health nurses may work with managed care providers and programs sponsored by health maintenance organizations.

As with almost all health care professions today, community health nurses spend a great deal of time keeping records and charts and documenting the services they provide in order to meet insurance, government, and Medicare requirements.

REQUIREMENTS

High School

To prepare for a career in nursing, take as many classes in science (especially biology and human anatomy), mathematics, computer science, psychology, and health as possible. English and speech classes will help you develop your communication skills.

Postsecondary Training

Nurses who specialize in a specific nursing field such as a community health nurse must first become registered nurses. (See "Registered Nurses.") Many community health nurses are required to have some general nursing experience, since they may be required to work with patients with a wide range of health problems. Entry-level requirements depend on the employing agency and the availability of nurses in that specialty and geographical region. Nurses who wish to specialize in community health care may choose to attend graduate school.

Certification or Licensing

Certification is a voluntary process. However, having credentials is a sign of competency and experience in nursing and may make the difference when applying for a job. Certification for community health nurses is available through the American Nurses Credentialing Center. Requirements for certification include holding a current nursing license, having a certain amount of professional experience, and passing the certification exam.

To practice in any of the 50 states and the District of Columbia, nurses must have graduated from an accredited program and pass a national licensing exam.

Other Requirements

Community health nurses should feel comfortable working with all ages and people from all cultural backgrounds. Good communication skills are essential, including the ability to listen and respond to

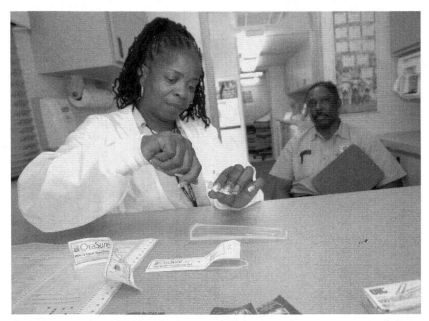

A community health nurse sets up an HIV test in the exam room of the Atlantic City (N.J.) Health Department's mobile van. *(Mary Godleski, AP Photo)*

the patient's needs. Flexibility is also a requirement, since duties vary greatly from hour to hour and day to day. Community health nurses must be able to work independently, have good organizational skills, and also have the ability to supervise aides and other support people.

EXPLORING

You can learn more about this field by reading books on careers in nursing, surfing the Web for information on nursing, and talking with your high school counselor, school nurse, or local public health nurse. You might also consider visiting your local hospital or clinic to observe the work of nurses.

EMPLOYERS

Community health nurses are employed by schools, correctional facilities, homeless shelters, elder care facilities, maternal and well-baby clinics, hospitals, managed care facilities, long-term care facilities, clinics, industry, private homes, camps, and government agencies.

STARTING OUT

Registered nurses may apply for employment directly to hospitals, nursing homes, companies, and government agencies that hire nurses. Jobs can also be obtained through school career services offices, by signing up with employment agencies specializing in placement of nursing personnel, or through the state employment office. Other sources of jobs include nurses' associations, professional journals, newspaper want ads, and Internet job sites.

ADVANCEMENT

Administrative and supervisory positions in the nursing field go to nurses who have earned at least the bachelor of science degree in nursing. Nurses with many years of experience who are graduates of the diploma program may achieve supervisory positions, but requirements for such promotions have become more difficult in recent years and in many cases require at least the bachelor of science in nursing degree.

EARNINGS

According to the U.S. Department of Labor (DOL), registered nurses (a group including community health nurses) had a median yearly income of $63,750 in 2009. The lowest paid 10 percent earned less than $43,970 annually, while the middle 50 percent earned between $52,520 and $77,970 per year. The top paid 10 percent of registered nurses earned more than $93,700 annually.

Salary is determined by many factors, including nursing specialty, education, place of employment, geographical location, and work experience. Flexible schedules are available for most full-time nurses. Employers usually provide health and life insurance, and some offer educational reimbursements and year-end bonuses to their full-time staff.

WORK ENVIRONMENT

Working environments vary depending on the community health nurse's responsibilities. Some community health nurses may work in clean, well-lighted buildings in upscale communities, while others may find themselves working in remote, underdeveloped areas that have poor living conditions. Personal safety may be an issue at times. Some community health nurses may also work overseas in government or private enterprises.

All nursing careers have some health and disease risks; however, adherence to health and safety guidelines greatly minimizes the chance of contracting infectious diseases such as hepatitis and AIDS. Medical knowledge and good safety measures are also needed to limit the nurse's exposure to toxic chemicals, radiation, and other hazards.

OUTLOOK

Nursing specialties will be in great demand in the coming years. The DOL lists nursing as one of the occupations predicted to have the largest number of new jobs. The DOL projects that employment for registered nurses will grow much faster than the average for all careers through 2018. In addition to the need for nurses to fill new jobs, there will also be the need for those to replace nurses who leave the field for retirement or other work.

The outlook for community health nurses is excellent. The Administration on Aging reports that in 2000, the senior population (those 65 and over) was approximately 35 million. This figure is expected to rise steadily and the number of seniors living in 2030 will be approximately 71.5 million. As our population grows older, the need for community-based nursing will increase. In addition, managed care organizations will continue to need community health nurses to provide health promotion and disease prevention programs to their subscribers.

FOR MORE INFORMATION

For information on nursing education and careers, contact the following organizations:

American Association of Colleges of Nursing
One Dupont Circle, NW, Suite 530
Washington, DC 20036-1135
Tel: 202-463-6930
http://www.aacn.nche.edu

Association of Community Health Nursing Educators
10200 West 44th Avenue, Suite 304
Wheat Ridge, CO 80033-2840
Tel: 303-422-0769
E-mail: achne@resourcecenter.com
http://www.achne.org

For information on certification, contact
American Nurses Credentialing Center
8515 Georgia Avenue, Suite 400
Silver Spring, MD 20910-3492
Tel: 800-284-2378
http://www.nursecredentialing.org

For information on public health careers, contact
American Public Health Association
800 I Street, NW
Washington, DC 20001-3710
Tel: 202-777-2742
http://www.apha.org

For career information, contact
Visiting Nurse Associations of America
900 19th Street, NW, Suite 200
Washington, DC 20006-2122
Tel: 202-384-1420
E-mail: vnaa@vnaa.org
http://www.vnaa.org

Critical Care Nurses

OVERVIEW

Critical care nurses are specialized nurses who provide highly skilled direct patient care to critically ill patients needing intense medical treatment. Critical care nurses work not only in intensive care units (ICU) and cardiac care units (CCU) of hospitals, but also in the emergency departments, post-anesthesia recovery units, pediatric intensive care units, burn units, and neonatal intensive care units of medical facilities, as well as in other units that treat critically ill patients. More than 500,000 nurses who care for acutely and critically ill patients are members of the American Association of Critical-Care Nurses (AACN).

HISTORY

There has always been a need for nurses to care for critically ill or injured patients, but, in the past, this type of care was provided by traditional nurses. As medical care grew more complicated as a result of technological advances and breakthroughs in treatment options, it became clear that special intensive care units were needed in hospitals. The first intensive care units were created in American hospitals in the 1950s. The specialized career of critical care nurse emerged at this time as demand for nurses with specialized training to work in these units grew. The field greatly expanded in the 1960s as cardiac care units were established in hospitals. In 1969, the AACN was founded to help represent the professional interests of critical care nurses.

QUICK FACTS

School Subjects
Biology
Chemistry

Personal Skills
Helping/teaching
Technical/scientific

Work Environment
Primarily indoors
Primarily one location

Minimum Education Level
Some postsecondary training

Salary Range
$43,970 to $67,740 to
$93,700+

Certification or Licensing
Recommended (certification)
Required by all states
(licensing)

Outlook
Much faster than the average

DOT
075

GOE
14.02.01

NOC
3152

O*NET-SOC
29-1111.03

THE JOB

Critical care nursing is a very challenging job. Because medical facilities employ critical care nurses who work in various units, their job responsibilities vary; however, their main responsibility is providing highly skilled medical and postsurgical care for critically ill patients. Critical care nurses may be assigned one or two patients that they care for as opposed to being involved in the care of several patients.

Brandon Frady, a registered nurse and a certified critical care nurse, works in the pediatrics intensive care unit of an Atlanta children's hospital. He works as a bedside nurse and as a relief charge nurse, meaning that he is not only responsible for caring for his patients, but he is also in charge of the administration of the ward.

Frady is also part of the ground transport team that transports critically ill or injured children within a 150-mile radius to their center. "We are the cutting edge hospital for pediatric health care," says Frady. "We care for very sick children here and our skills are challenged on a daily basis."

Critical care nursing requires keeping up with the latest medical technology and research as well as medical treatments and procedures. "There is something new to learn every day," Frady says. "We have to learn to operate very high-tech machines, and we are frequently tested on their use and operation. Plus, we need to know the latest research and treatments available for acutely ill children."

Critical care nursing is a very intense nursing specialty. Patients require constant care and monitoring, says Frady. "Many hospitals are requiring nurses to work 12-hour shifts, which can be very exhausting."

In many cases, critical care nurses are confronted with situations that require them to act immediately on the patients' behalf. The nurse must be a patient advocate, meaning that the nurse must help the patients receive the best possible care and also respect their wishes. They must also provide support and education to the patients and their families.

"Although it can be an emotionally draining job, it can also be very rewarding to know that I helped the child and family get through their medical crisis," Frady says. "It is especially satisfying when they come back later and thank you for what you have done. The job has a lot of satisfaction."

REQUIREMENTS

High School

To prepare for a career in nursing, take as many classes in science (especially biology and human anatomy), mathematics, computer science, psychology, and health as possible. English and speech classes will help you develop your communication skills.

Postsecondary Training
Critical care nurses must be registered nurses. (See "Registered Nurses.") Entry-level requirements to become a critical care nurse depend on the institution, its size, who it serves, and the availability of nurses in that specialty and geographical region. Usually nurses must have some bedside nursing experience before entering the critical care nursing field. However, some hospitals are developing graduate internship and orientation programs that allow new graduates to enter this specialty.

Certification or Licensing
There are more than five critical care nursing certification programs available through the AACN. The American Nurses Credentialing Center also provides certification to critical care nurses. Some institutions may require certification as a critical care nurse. In addition, registered nurses, regardless of specialty, must be licensed in order to practice in all 50 states and the District of Columbia. Licensing is obtained by passing a national exam.

Other Requirements
Critical care nurses should like working in a fast-paced environment that requires lifelong learning. This is a very intense nursing field, and nurses should be able to make critical decisions quickly and intelligently. New medical technology is constantly being developed and implemented. Critical care nurses should be technically inclined and able to learn how to operate new medical equipment without feeling intimidated.

Critical care nurses must be able to deal with major life and death crises. Because of the seriousness of their loved one's illness, family members and friends may be difficult to deal with and the nurse must display patience, understanding, and composure during these emotional times. The nurse must be able to communicate with the family and explain medical terminology and procedures to the patient and family so they can understand what is being done and why.

Continuing education is a must in order to stay informed of new treatment options and procedures.

EXPLORING
There are many ways to explore nursing careers. You can visit nursing Web sites, read books on careers in nursing, or talk with your

Patient Advocacy

According to the AACN, the critical care nurse is first and foremost a patient advocate. In this role, critical care nurses do the following:

- Respect the rights of the patient or the patient's designated surrogate to make informed decisions.
- Educate and support the patient's designated surrogate in their decision-making process.
- Intervene when it is in the best interests of the patient to do so.
- Help the patient obtain all necessary care.
- Respect the rights, values, and beliefs of the patient and represent the patient accordingly.
- Intercede for patients who cannot speak for themselves in situations that require immediate action.
- Act as liaison between the patient, the patient's family and support network, and other health care providers.

high school counselor or teacher about the career or ask them to set up a talk by a critical care nurse.

If you are already a nursing student, you might consider becoming a student member of the AACN. This will give you access to *Critical Care Nurse, The American Journal of Critical Care*, and other association publications that discuss issues related to critical care nursing.

EMPLOYERS

More than 500,000 nurses who care for acutely and critically ill patients are members of the American Association of Critical-Care Nurses. Contrary to previously held beliefs that critical care nurses work only in intensive care units or cardiac care units of hospitals, today's critical care nurses work in the emergency departments, post-anesthesia recovery units, pediatric intensive care units, burn units, and neonatal intensive care units of medical facilities, as well as in other units that treat critically ill patients.

STARTING OUT

You must first become a registered nurse before you can work as a critical care nurse. Aspiring registered nurses must complete one of the three kinds of educational programs and pass the licensing examination. Registered nurses may apply for employment directly to hospitals, nursing homes, and companies and government agencies that hire nurses. Jobs can also be obtained through school career services offices, by signing up with employment agencies specializing in placement of nursing personnel, or through the state employment office. Other sources of jobs include nurses' associations, professional journals, and newspaper want ads. The AACN also has job listings on its Web site, http://www.aacn.org.

ADVANCEMENT

Administrative and supervisory positions in the nursing field go to nurses who have earned at least the bachelor of science degree in nursing. Nurses with many years of experience who are graduates of the diploma program may achieve supervisory positions, but requirements for such promotions have become more difficult in recent years and in many cases require at least the bachelor of science in nursing degree.

EARNINGS

Salary is determined by many factors, including certification and education, place of employment, shift worked, geographical location, and work experience. The U.S. Department of Labor (DOL) reports the median annual salary for registered nurses (which includes critical care nurses) employed by hospitals was $67,740 in 2009. The lowest paid 10 percent of all registered nurses made less than $43,970 per year, and the highest paid 10 percent made more than $93,700. Since critical care nurses must be registered nurses and also have additional training, their salaries should be higher on average than registered nurses who are not in the critical care area.

Flexible schedules and part-time employment opportunities are available for most nurses. Employers usually provide health and life insurance, and some offer educational reimbursements and year-end bonuses to their full-time staff.

WORK ENVIRONMENT

Most critical care nurses work in hospitals in the intensive care unit (ICU), the emergency department, the operating room, or some other specialty unit. Most hospital environments are clean and well lighted. Inner city hospitals may be in a less than desirable location and safety may be an issue. Generally, critical care nurses who wish to advance in their careers will find themselves working in larger hospitals or medical centers in major cities.

All nursing careers have some health and disease risks; however, adherence to health and safety guidelines greatly minimizes the chance of contracting infectious diseases such as hepatitis and AIDS. Medical knowledge and good safety measures are also needed to limit the nurse's exposure to toxic chemicals, radiation, and other hazards.

OUTLOOK

Nursing specialties will be in great demand in the future. The DOL estimates the employment of all registered nurses will grow much faster than the average for all careers through 2018. According to the AACN, a growing number of hospitals are experiencing a shortage of critical care nurses. Many hospitals needing critical care nurses are offering incentives such as sign-on bonuses. The most critical shortages are in areas that require nurses with experience and highly specialized skills. The highest increase in demand is for those critical care nurses who specialize in a specific area of care, such as cardiovascular ICU, pediatric and neonatal ICU, and open-heart recovery units. Job opportunities vary across the country and may be available in all geographic areas and in large and small hospitals.

FOR MORE INFORMATION

For information on nursing careers and accredited programs, contact
American Association of Colleges of Nursing
One Dupont Circle, NW, Suite 530
Washington, DC 20036-1135
Tel: 202-463-6930
http://www.aacn.nche.edu

For information on certification and fact sheets on critical care nursing, contact
American Association of Critical-Care Nurses
101 Columbia
Aliso Viejo, CA 92656-4109
Tel: 800-899-2226
E-mail: info@aacn.org
http://www.aacn.org

For information on certification, contact
American Nurses Credentialing Center
8515 Georgia Avenue, Suite 400
Silver Spring, MD 20910-3492
Tel: 800-284-2378
http://www.nursecredentialing.org

═══ INTERVIEW ═══

Michelle Legg, RN, BSN, CCRN, is a critical care nurse in the Coronary Intensive Care Unit at Virginia Commonwealth University Medical Center. She discussed her career with the editors of Careers in Focus: Nursing.

Q. How long have you worked in the field? What made you want to enter this career?

A. I have been a registered nurse for four-and-a-half years and worked for a year prior to that as a care partner. I wanted a challenging career where I helped people and was constantly busy, while learning new information each day.

Q. Can you describe a typical day in your life as a critical care nurse?

A. Each day is different. Some days can be typical with caring for two patients who are having heart attacks. Other days we can be providing comfort care for the family and palliative care for our patient. On a separate (or even sometimes the same) day, we can be battling for a patient with cardiogenic shock and/or sepsis. We are managing the patient's illness and watching for signs of distress or deterioration so that the doctor can be notified immediately and action taken to prevent a worsening condition. We have to be very flexible, especially on our unit where we board overflow patients from cardiac surgery, medical respiratory, surgical/trauma, and neuroscience intensive care units. Usually, I will be in charge once a week to once every other week. We have staffing issues consistently. Because our unit is so versatile, some days we are overflowing with patients without enough nurses, while other days (very few in the last six months or so) we have [a sufficient number of] nurses and very few patients. Our unit is like a revolving door, as well, so as soon as one patient is moved to a step-down unit, we have another coming in. We are not allowed to staff for our "flex up" bed; however, we are expected to take a patient in that bed without having staff to care for them. So, it can be stressful, especially if you are the charge nurse, trying to care for your patients while also advocating for your unit to get the assistance it needs to take care of the patients. Some days, I serve as a rapid response nurse. Recently, because of staffing issues on our unit or others within the Heart Center, the rapid response nurse has also had to take an assignment, which can also be stressful. That said, our nurses pull together as a team and get the job done. Somehow everything comes together and works out.

Q. What are the most important personal and professional qualities for critical care nurses?

A. It is important to dress in clean, presentable scrubs, have a smile on your face, and leave home issues away from the bedside. This also means not talking on the phone or texting in your patients' rooms. For me, if I have a particularly difficult patient, who isn't satisfied with anything I seem to do to make their life better, I remember that they are not feeling well and don't really want to be there and shrug it off. It is also important to treat your colleagues with respect and mind your manners and leave attitudes at the door. For us, teamwork is essential.

Q. What are some of the pros and cons of your job?

A. Pros: Helping people, gratification, working [only] three days a week, and constantly learning new information.
Cons: 12-hour shifts can be long, rotating shifts.

Q. What advice would you give to young people who are interested in the field?

A. Shadow a nurse for a day and ask all the important questions. Make sure you understand what nursing entails before you go through school and start working, only to realize there is so much more involved than the image that is portrayed in the media or passed on generation by generation. It's not just about bedpans. You constantly need to be on your toes to recognize signs of illness and think fast to curtail deterioration of the patient and to advocate for them.

Emergency Nurses

OVERVIEW

Emergency nurses provide highly skilled direct patient care to those who need emergency treatment for an illness or injury. Emergency nurses incorporate all the specialties of nursing. They care for infant, pediatric, adult, and elderly patients with a broad spectrum of medical needs.

HISTORY

Nurses have provided emergency care to critically ill or injured patients since the first medical professionals cared for people. In the United States, hospital emergency departments were established in the early 1900s. Emergency nurses were the linchpins of these departments, but often were overshadowed by emergency room physicians. In 1970, the Emergency Department Nurses Association was founded to represent the professional interests of emergency nurses. In 1985, its name was changed to the Emergency Nurses Association (ENA). Today, the ENA has more than 30,000 members in more than 32 countries.

THE JOB

The main responsibility of emergency nurses is to provide highly skilled emer-

gency medical care for patients. Although emergency nursing is its own nursing specialty, it incorporates almost every other nursing specialty in the profession. Emergency nurses deal with pregnant women, newborn babies, patients with cancer, children, accident victims, AIDS patients, Alzheimer's patients, the elderly, cardiac arrest patients, and psychologically disturbed and violent people.

The emergency ward of a hospital is a web of activity as nurses and doctors discuss cases, review patient files, and confer with other health care professionals via telephone. *(Alexandra Boulat, AP Photo/VII)*

Emergency care can range from giving general nursing care to someone with a severe case of the flu, to performing life-saving procedures.

When a patient enters the emergency facility, the nurses must first assess the patient and determine the immediacy of the illness or injury. This includes a quick preliminary diagnosis and assessment of the patient's overall condition. They talk to the patient and family. They also record vital signs and observe the patient's symptoms or check for injuries that may not be readily visible.

Emergency nurses must prioritize their patients' needs, especially if it is a triage situation, such as a disaster or accident involving a number of people who require treatment. They must be able to stabilize the patient; prepare the patient for emergency testing, laboratory procedures, or surgery; and perform resuscitation, if necessary. In many instances the nurse will have to perform initial treatment until a doctor can see the patient. This may include setting up or using high-tech medical equipment.

In many cases, emergency nurses are confronted with situations that require them to act immediately, independently, and confidently. But, they must be a good team player, working with other medical, administrative, and law enforcement personnel in what can become a very tense and emotional situation.

Nursing Resources on the Web

American Assembly for Men in Nursing
http://www.aamn.org

Cybernurse.com
http://www.cybernurse.com

Discover Nursing
http://www.discovernursing.com

ExceptionalNurse.com
http://www.exceptionalnurse.com

How Stuff Works: How Emergency Rooms Work
http://people.howstuffworks.com/emergency-room.htm

InnerBody: Your Guide to Human Anatomy Online
http://www.innerbody.com/htm/body.html

Often emergency nurses must be patient advocates, meaning that they must help the patient receive the best possible care and also respect the patient's wishes regarding treatment. Nurses must be in touch with the family during the emergency crisis and help them deal with their emotions and fears.

Not only are emergency nurses required to attend to the physical needs of patients, they may be involved in crisis intervention in some cases such as homelessness, sexual assault, domestic violence, or child abuse.

Emergency nurses must also act as educators. Many people who are seen in emergency care facilities do not have access to follow-up care so nurses must educate their patients about self-care when they are discharged. This may include showing them how to care for their wounds or injuries or recommending lifestyle changes, if necessary, to adapt to their conditions or plans of treatment.

Flight nurses are specialized emergency nurses who care for critically ill or injured patients who are being transported from accident scenes to a medical care facility or from one hospital to another.

REQUIREMENTS

High School

Take as many science (especially biology and human anatomy), mathematics, psychology, computer science, and health classes as you can in high school. Other recommended courses include computer science, English, and speech.

Postsecondary Training

Emergency nurses must be registered nurses. Entry-level requirements to become an emergency nurse depend on the state, the institution, its size, who it serves, and the availability of nurses in that specialty and geographical region. Usually nurses must have some nursing experience before entering the emergency nursing field.

Certification or Licensing

Some employers may require emergency room nurses to be certified. Certification is available through the Board of Certification for Emergency Nursing and requires recertification every four years.

All states and the District of Columbia require a license to practice nursing. To obtain a license, graduates of approved nursing schools must pass a national examination. Nurses may be licensed by more than one state. In some states, continuing education is a condition for license renewal.

Other Requirements

Emergency room nurses should like working in a fast-paced environment that requires lifelong learning. This is a very intense nursing field and nurses should be able to make critical decisions quickly and intelligently. New medical technology is constantly being developed and implemented, and emergency care nurses should be technically inclined and skilled in operating medical equipment.

Emergency nurses must be able to deal with major life and death crises. Because of the suddenness and perhaps seriousness of their loved one's illness, family members and friends may be difficult to deal with and the nurse must display patience, understanding, and composure during these emotional times. The nurse must be able to communicate with the family and explain medical terminology and procedures to the patient and family so they can understand what is being done and why.

Emergency nursing is a very intense nursing specialty, as patients require immediate attention, constant care, and monitoring. Many facilities are requiring nurses to work 12-hour shifts, which can be very exhausting. In addition, emergency nurses are often on call in the event of a disaster, severe accident, or some other situation where additional staff may be needed.

EXPLORING

If a career in emergency nursing appeals to you, learn more about the job by experiencing health care work first hand. Volunteer at a local hospital or nursing home to interact with patients and to talk to nursing professionals on the job. Observe them at work and ask how they got started in nursing. You can learn a lot from their experience.

In addition, visit your local school or neighborhood library to research nursing and other health care careers. Read books and medical periodicals about the latest developments in the industry and how to get started on the career path.

EMPLOYERS

Many emergency nurses work in hospital emergency rooms or emergency care centers. They are also employed by managed care facilities, long-term care facilities, government agencies, camps, government institutions, corporations, businesses, correctional institutions, and other health care institutions.

STARTING OUT

Emergency nurses must first become registered nurses by completing one of the three kinds of educational programs and passing the licensing examination. Registered nurses may apply for employment directly to hospitals, nursing homes, and companies and government agencies that hire nurses. Jobs can also be obtained through school career services offices, by signing up with employment agencies specializing in placement of nursing personnel, or through the state employment office. Other sources of jobs include nurses' associations, professional journals, career and social networking Web sites, and newspaper want ads.

ADVANCEMENT

Administrative and supervisory positions in the nursing field go to nurses who have earned at least the bachelor of science degree in nursing. Nurses with many years of experience who are graduates of the diploma program may achieve supervisory positions, but requirements for such promotions have become more difficult in recent years and in many cases require at least the bachelor of science in nursing degree.

EARNINGS

According to the U.S. Department of Labor, registered nurses earned a median of $63,750 annually in 2009. The lowest paid 10 percent earned less than $43,970, while the middle 50 percent earned between $52,520 and $77,970. The top paid 10 percent made more than $93,700 a year. According to Salary.com, staff nurses in emergency rooms earned salaries that ranged from less than $52,640 to $77,921 or more in November 2010. However, emergency nurses in certain areas may earn more.

Salary is determined by many factors, including nursing specialty, education, place of employment, shift worked, geographical location, and work experience. Flexible schedules and part-time employment opportunities are available for most nurses.

Employers offer a variety of benefit packages, which can include any of the following: paid holidays, vacations, and sick days; personal days; medical, dental, and life insurance; profit-sharing plans; 401(k) plans; retirement and pension plans; and educational assistance programs.

WORK ENVIRONMENT

Camps, government institutions, corporations, businesses, correctional institutions, and other health care institutions may employ emergency nurses. Many emergency nurses work in hospital emergency rooms or emergency care centers. Most hospital and institutional environments are clean and well lit. Inner city facilities and hospitals may be in less than desirable locations and safety may be an issue. Generally, emergency nurses who wish to advance in their careers will find themselves working in larger facilities in major cities.

All nursing careers have some health and disease risks; however, adherence to health and safety guidelines greatly minimizes the chance of contracting infectious diseases such as hepatitis and AIDS. Medical knowledge and good safety measures are also needed to limit the nurse's exposure to toxic chemicals, radiation, and other hazards.

OUTLOOK

Nursing specialties will be in great demand in the future. The U.S. Bureau of Labor Statistics projects that employment for registered nurses will grow much faster than the average for all occupations through 2018. There will continue to be a strong need for emergency nurses to care for patients who are ill or injured and who need immediate care.

FOR MORE INFORMATION

For information on a career as a flight nurse, contact
Air and Surface Transport Nurses Association
7995 East Prentice Avenue, Suite 100
Greenwood Village CO 80111-2707
Tel: 800-897-6362
http://www.astna.org

For information on nursing education and careers, contact
American Association of Colleges of Nursing
One Dupont Circle, NW, Suite 530
Washington, DC 20036-1135
Tel: 202-463-6930
http://www.aacn.nche.edu

For information on emergency nursing careers and certification, contact
Emergency Nurses Association
915 Lee Street
Des Plaines, IL 60016-6569
Tel: 800-900-9659
E-mail: enainfo@ena.org
http://www.ena.org

Forensic Nurses

QUICK FACTS

School Subjects
Biology
Chemistry
Health

Personal Skills
Helping/teaching
Technical/scientific

Work Environment
Primarily indoors
Primarily multiple locations

Minimum Education Level
Some postsecondary training

Salary Range
$43,970 to $63,750 to
$93,700+

Certification or Licensing
Voluntary (certification)
Required by all states
(licensing)

Outlook
Much faster than the average

DOT
075

GOE
14.02.01

NOC
3152

O*NET-SOC
29-1111.00

OVERVIEW

Forensic nursing is a relatively new and expanding field of nursing that combines nursing skills with investigative skills. *Forensic nurses* are trained to work with victims, suspects, and evidence of crimes, and work in a variety of settings. They may have additional titles specific to their occupation. Forensic nurses are registered nurses who have received additional training that prepares them for work in the field. There are approximately 2.6 million registered nurses in the United States. Only a small percentage of registered nurses specialize in forensic nursing.

HISTORY

Modern ideas about hospitals and nursing as a profession did not develop until the 19th century. The life and work of Florence Nightingale were a strong influence on the profession's development. Nightingale, who came from a wealthy, upper-class British family, dedicated her life to improving conditions in hospitals, beginning in an army hospital during the Crimean War. In the United States, many of Nightingale's ideas were put into practice for the care of the wounded during the Civil War. The care, however, was provided by concerned individuals who nursed rather than by trained nurses. They had not received the kind of training that is required for nurses today.

The first school of nursing in the United States was founded in Boston in 1873. In 1938, New York State passed the first state law to require that practical nurses be licensed. After the 1938 law was passed, a movement began to have organized training programs that would assure new standards in the field. The role and training of nurses have undergone radical changes since the first schools were opened.

Nurses have been working with victims of abuse and sexual assault for years, but it was not until 1992 that the term *forensic nurse* was used to describe nurses in this specialty. Seventy-two nurses met at a professional conference hosted by the Sexual Assault Resource Service and the University of Minnesota School of Nursing in Minneapolis, Minnesota, to discuss the field of sexual assault nursing. They quickly realized that they had much in common and that they should form a professional association to represent their interests. The International Association of Forensic Nurses (IAFN) was incorporated in 1993. In 1996, the American Association of Nurses recognized forensic nursing as a specialty of nursing. Today, the IAFN has more than 3,000 members in 24 countries. The association's members work not only in sexual assault examination positions, but in any situations in which people have been abused or an accident has occurred that has caused injury or loss of life.

THE JOB

Forensic nurses use a combination of skills to meet multiple purposes, often serving not only as nurses, but as crime solvers and advocates for victims, too. They are employed in a variety of settings. They may work in hospitals (particularly in emergency rooms) or other health care facilities, correctional institutions, the offices of medical examiners and coroners, psychiatric facilities, insurance agencies, social service agencies . . . the list goes on. In general, anywhere that a registered nurse might work is a setting in which the skills of a forensic nurse will likely be of use, especially if it is a place where victims or suspects in a crime or accident may be investigated or treated.

In addition to performing general nursing duties, forensic nurses are likely to be involved with additional tasks related to investigations of accidents or crimes. These duties include observing the victims of (and sometimes the scene of) an accident or crime for potential evidence—forensic nurses are generally better trained than other nurses to spot signs of abuse or trauma. They may also examine suspected perpetrators of crimes. A forensic nurse must carefully collect, document, and preserve any evidence they find for any future legal proceedings. Many forensic nurses are called on to provide testimony in court.

There are several specialties in the field of forensic nursing. One of the largest areas of specialization pertains to sexual assault examination. Forensic nurses trained in this area often have an additional title, such as *sexual assault nurse examiner* (SANE), *sexual assault examiner* (SAE), *sexual assault forensic examiner* (SAFE), or *forensic nurse examiner* (FNE). As most of these titles imply, SANEs, SAEs, SAFEs, and FNEs work with survivors of sexual assault. They typically interview the survivors, obtaining their medical history and a thorough account of the assault. The forensic nurse then performs a physical examination, looking for any signs of the assault. Although sometimes signs of trauma are clearly evident, in many cases they are internal and not easily visible without careful examination and special supplies and equipment. Evidence is carefully obtained, documented, and preserved: this may range from collecting fluids, hairs, textiles, or other physical bits of evidence, to recording evidence of trauma, such as taking photographs of bruising or lacerations to the victim's body. Later, the forensic nurse may be called upon to testify in a legal proceeding related to the assault.

Trauma nurses with forensic nursing training typically work in the emergency rooms of hospitals. Their functions are similar to those of SANEs and the related nurses discussed above, but they have a much broader mandate, as they come in contact with many patients and focus on those who may be the victims or perpetrators of domestic violence, other types of abuse, and crimes. *Trauma forensic nurses* examine patients and preserve and/or document evidence of the injuries caused by the abuse or crime, or, in the case of a suspected perpetrator, any evidence indicating he or she committed the abuse or crime. They also identify patients who may have attempted suicide or are displaying psychiatric symptoms and help direct them to the mental health care they need.

Forensic nurse investigators are involved in death investigations. They are employed by offices of coroners or medical examiners and work alongside law enforcement personnel at the scene of a death. They may examine the deceased individual and investigate the physical location of and the circumstances surrounding the death. They may also assist in conducting autopsies.

Another area of specialization is legal consulting. Forensic nurses in this area may have an additional title, typically *legal nurse consultant* (LNC). LNCs are much more involved in the legal aspects of investigations than other forensic nurses. They work on a range of cases—usually civil rather than criminal—that deal with such issues as medical malpractice, personal injury, wrongful death, or worker's compensation. (See the article "Legal Nurse Consultants" for more information on this career.)

Other forensic nurses work with specific groups of people, such as geriatric, pediatric, incarcerated, or mentally ill populations, focusing on investigating the injuries or deaths caused by the abuse or crimes affecting those groups. In addition, forensic nurses working with mentally ill populations also may be responsible for assessing a person's level of competency, whether it be at the present time, what it might be in the future, or trying to determining what it was at a previous point in time, such as during a criminal incident.

REQUIREMENTS

High School
In order to become a forensic nurse you will first need to become a registered nurse. To prepare for training as a registered nurse, you should take high school mathematics and science courses, including biology, chemistry, and physics. Health courses will also be helpful. English and speech courses should not be neglected because you must be able to communicate well with patients. Psychology classes will be especially useful for aspiring forensic nurses because they often work with people who have been the victims of a crime.

Postsecondary Training
There are three basic kinds of training programs that you may choose from to become a registered nurse: associate's degree, diploma, and bachelor's degree. The choice of which of the three training programs to pursue depends on your career goals. A bachelor's degree in nursing is required for most supervisory or administrative positions, for jobs in public health agencies, and for admission to graduate nursing programs. There are approximately 710 bachelor's degree programs in nursing in the United States. A bachelor's degree in nursing requires four (in some cases, five) years to complete. The graduate of this program receives a bachelor of science in nursing (BSN) degree. The associate degree in nursing (ADN) is awarded after completion of a two-year study program that is usually offered by a junior or community college. There are approximately 850 ADN programs in the United States. You receive hospital training at cooperating hospitals in the general vicinity of the community college. The diploma program, which usually lasts three years, is conducted by hospitals and independent schools, although the number of these programs is declining. At the conclusion of each of these programs, you become

A forensic clinical nurse specialist testifies about sexual assault testing procedures during a trial. *(Marty Caivano, AP Photo/Pool)*

a graduate nurse, but not, however, a registered nurse. To obtain the RN designation you must pass a licensing examination required in all states.

Courses in forensic nursing are often offered as electives during undergraduate training. It is a good idea to take as many of these as possible while an undergraduate.

The next step to becoming a forensic nurse is earning a graduate degree in forensic nursing. The International Association of Forensic Nurses offers a list of colleges and universities that offer degrees in forensic nursing at its Web site, http://www.iafn.org.

According to The Forensic Nurse Web site (http://www.theforensic nurse.com), forensic nurses must have "successfully completed a formal didactic educational program in forensic nursing . . . which included a minimum of 40 contact hours in the core areas of forensic nursing. These core areas include the history of forensic nursing; the forensic nursing process; violence and victimology; injury identification, interpretation, and documentation; criminalistics and forensic science; and nursing and the interdisciplinary process with law enforcement/and legal process."

Certification or Licensing

Voluntary certification is available for a variety of registered nursing specialties. The International Association of Forensic Nurses offers the following voluntary certifications to forensic nurses: SANE-A (for sexual assault nurse examiners of adults and adolescents) and SANE-P (for sexual assault nurse examiners that care for pediatric and adolescent populations). Applicants must satisfy experience requirements and pass an examination. Certification must be renewed every three years.

The International Association of Forensic Nurses is currently working with the American Nurse Credentialing Center (http://www.nursecredentialing.org) to develop the advanced practice forensic nurse portfolio credential.

The American College of Forensic Examiners offers the voluntary certified forensic nurse designation to those who satisfy experience and education requirements and pass an examination.

Certification as a legal nurse consultant certified is voluntary and is available through the American Legal Nurse Consultant Certification Board. This credential demonstrates that the legal nurse consultant has met practice experience requirements and has passed an examination testing all areas of legal nurse consulting. The certificate is renewed every five years through continuing education or reexamination and continued practice in the specialty.

All states and the District of Columbia require a license to practice nursing. To obtain a license, graduates of approved nursing schools must pass a national examination. Nurses may be licensed by more than one state. In some states, continuing education is a condition for license renewal. Different titles require different education and training levels.

Other Requirements

You should have a strong desire to help others, especially those who may experience fear or anger as a result of being abused or a victim of a crime. Patience, compassion, objectivity, and calmness are qualities needed by anyone working in this career. In addition, you must have excellent observational and communication skills, be detail oriented, and be able to give directions as well as follow instructions and work as part of a health care team. Anyone interested in becoming a forensic nurse should also have a strong desire to continue learning because new tests, procedures, and technologies are constantly being developed.

EXPLORING

You can explore your general interest in nursing in a number of ways. Read books on careers in nursing and talk with high school counselors, school nurses, and local public health nurses. Visit hospitals to observe the work and talk with hospital personnel to learn more about the daily activities of nursing staff.

Some hospitals now have extensive volunteer service programs in which high school students may work after school, on weekends, or during vacations in order to both render a valuable service and to explore their interests. There are other volunteer work experiences available with the Red Cross or community health services. Camp counseling jobs sometimes offer related experiences. Some schools offer participation in Future Nurses programs.

The Internet is full of resources about nursing. Check out Discover Nursing (http://www.discovernursing.com), Nursing Net (http://www.nursingnet.org), and the American Nurses Association's Nursing World (http://www.nursingworld.org).

You won't be able to explore work as a forensic nurse directly, but there are still many ways to learn about the field. In addition to the general suggestions made earlier about exploring nursing, you can also read books about forensic nursing, such as *Forensic Nurse: The New Role of the Nurse in Law Enforcement*, by Serita Stevens (New York: St. Martin's Press, 2008) and visit Web sites about forensic nursing, such as The Forensic Nurse (http://www .theforensicnurse.com). You should also ask your health teacher or school counselor to help arrange an information interview with a forensic nurse.

EMPLOYERS

Approximately 2.6 million registered nurses are employed in the United States, but only a very small percentage of RNs work as forensic nurses. Employers of forensic nurses include hospitals (particularly in emergency rooms) and other health care facilities, offices of medical examiners and coroners, correctional institutions, law firms, psychiatric facilities, insurance agencies, and social service agencies. Twenty percent of all nurses work part time.

STARTING OUT

The only way to become a registered nurse is through completion of one of the three kinds of educational programs, plus passing the licensing examination. Registered nurses may apply for employment directly to hospitals, nursing homes, home care agencies, temporary nursing agencies, companies, and government agencies that hire nurses. Jobs can also be obtained through school career services offices, by signing up with employment agencies specializing in placement of nursing personnel, or through state employment offices. Other sources of jobs include nurses' associations, professional journals, and newspaper want ads.

The International Association of Forensic Nurses provides job listings at its Web site, http://nurse.associationcareernetwork.com/Common/HomePage.aspx.

ADVANCEMENT

Increasingly, administrative and supervisory positions in the nursing field go to forensic nurses who have earned at least a bachelor of science in nursing. Forensic nurses with many years of experience who are graduates of a diploma program may achieve supervisory positions, but requirements for such promotions have become more difficult in recent years and in many cases require at least the BSN degree.

EARNINGS

Forensic nurses may earn a regular salary, be paid per case, or be paid by the hour. The U.S. Department of Labor (DOL) does not provide salary information for forensic nurses, but it does provide information on earnings for registered nurses. In 2009, registered nurses had median annual earnings of $63,750. Salaries ranged from less than $43,970 to more than $93,700. Those who worked at hospitals had mean annual earnings of $67,740. According to The Forensic Nurse Web site, forensic nurses may be paid anywhere from $150 to $400 per case. Other forensic nurses may receive hourly salaries that range from $25/hour to $100/hour or more.

Salaries for forensic nurses are determined by several factors: setting, education, and work experience. Most full-time forensic nurses are given flexible work schedules as well as health and life insurance; some are offered education reimbursement and year-end bonuses.

Many forensic nurses take advantage of overtime work and shift differentials. About 7 percent of all nurses hold more than one job.

Benefits for full-time workers include paid vacation, health, disability, life insurance, and retirement or pension plans.

WORK ENVIRONMENT

Most forensic nurses work in facilities that are clean and well lighted and where the temperature is controlled, although some work in rundown inner city hospitals in less-than-ideal conditions.

Forensic nurses spend much of their workday on their feet, either walking or standing. Assisting patients who have been sexually assaulted or otherwise abused, as well as working with criminal offenders, can be very stressful and exhausting. Despite this, forensic nurses must maintain their composure and focus on doing their jobs and helping crime victims receive justice.

Forensic nurses who work in hospital emergency rooms and clinics that handle sexual assault cases may be on call, which often involves being called to work on evenings and weekends. They may have to travel to the scene of a crime and to court to testify regarding their findings.

OUTLOOK

The nursing field is the largest of all health care occupations, and employment prospects for nurses are excellent. The DOL projects that employment for registered nurses will grow much faster than the average for all professions through 2018.

Opportunities should also be very strong for forensic nurses. This profession is growing quickly as a result of increases in crime. There is currently a shortage of experienced forensic nurses, which is creating demand for qualified professionals. Registered nurses with graduate degrees and/or certificates in forensic nursing will have the best employment prospects.

FOR MORE INFORMATION

For information about forensic nursing, contact
Academy of Forensic Nursing Science
Tel: 760-322-9925
E-mail: info@tafns.com
http://www.academyofforensicnursingscience.com

Visit the AACN Web site to access a list of member schools and to read the online pamphlet Your Nursing Career: A Look at the Facts.

American Association of Colleges of Nursing (AACN)
One Dupont Circle, Suite 530
Washington, DC 20036-1135
Tel: 202-463-6930
http://www.aacn.nche.edu

For information on certification and to read Getting Started in Legal Nurse Consulting: An Introduction to the Specialty, *visit the AALNC Web site.*

American Association of Legal Nurse Consultants (AALNC)
401 North Michigan Avenue
Chicago, IL 60611-4255
Tel: 877-402-2562
E-mail: info@aalnc.org
http://www.aalnc.org

For information on forensic science and certification, contact

American College of Forensic Examiners International
2750 East Sunshine Street
Springfield, MO 65804-2047
Tel: 800-423-9737
http://www.acfei.com

For information about opportunities as an RN, contact the following organizations:

American Nurses Association
8515 Georgia Avenue, Suite 400
Silver Spring, MD 20910-3492
Tel: 800-274-4262
http://www.nursingworld.org

American Society of Registered Nurses
1001 Bridgeway, Suite 233
Sausalito, CA 94965-2104
Tel: 415-331-2700
E-mail: office@asrn.org
http://www.asrn.org

Visit the association's Web site for information on educational programs, careers, and certification.

International Association of Forensic Nurses
1517 Ritchie Highway, Suite 208
Arnold, MD 21012-2323
Tel: 410-626-7805
E-mail: info@iafn.org
http://www.iafn.org

For information about state-approved programs and information on nursing, contact the following organizations:

National League for Nursing
61 Broadway, 33rd Floor
New York, NY 10006-2701
Tel: 212-363-5555
E-mail: generalinfo@nln.org
http://www.nln.org

National Organization for Associate Degree Nursing
7794 Grow Drive
Pensacola, FL 32514-7072
Tel: 850-484-6948
E-mail: noadn@dancyamc.com
https://www.noadn.org

Discover Nursing, sponsored by Johnson & Johnson Services Inc., provides information on nursing careers (including forensic nursing), nursing schools, and scholarships.

Discover Nursing
http://www.discovernursing.com

Geriatric Nurses

OVERVIEW

Geriatric nurses provide direct patient care to elderly people in their homes, or in hospitals, nursing homes, and clinics. The term *geriatrics* refers to the clinical aspects of aging and the overall health care of the aging population. Since older people tend to have different reactions to illness and disease than younger people, treating them has become a specialty.

HISTORY

The specialty of gerontology nursing started developing in the 20th century as people routinely began to live longer than in past generations. Healthier lifestyles, new medicines, and new medical procedures, among other things, contributed to this change in life span. And as more and more people lived longer, a growing number needed and wanted the expertise of health care professionals who are well versed in the needs and concerns of older people. Geriatric nurses are able to address the special health problems older people may face, such as serious chronic problems (heart disease or blood pressure illness), decreases in senses and physical agility (sight, hearing, balance) that lead to injuries from accidents, and the problems that may result from accidents (learning to walk again after a broken hip). They also care for patients in hospice programs who are in the final stages of a terminal illness.

The Administration on Aging reports that in 2000, the senior population (those 65 and over) was approximately 35 million. This figure is expected to rise steadily and the number of seniors living in

2030 will be approximately 71.5 million. Thus, health care services for seniors will continue to be a growing field.

THE JOB

Geriatric nurses focus primarily on caring for elderly patients. This care may be provided in an institution, in the home as a visiting nurse or hospice nurse, in a retirement community, in a doctor's office, in the hospital, or at wellness clinics in the community. Some geriatric nurses may also give health seminars or workshops to the elderly in the community, or they may be involved in research or pilot studies that deal with health and disease among the aging population.

Geriatric nurses can expect to perform many of the skills required of any nursing professional. Many nurses who specialize in other types of care, with the exception of pediatrics and obstetrics, almost always find themselves caring for the elderly as well.

There are many nursing specialties under the broad umbrella of geriatric nursing. The following paragraphs describe a few of them.

Home health care nurses, also called *visiting nurses*, provide home-based health care under the direction of a physician. They care for persons who may be recovering from an accident, illness, surgery, cancer, or childbirth. They may work for a community organization, a private health care provider, or they may be independent nurses who work on a contract basis.

While home health care nurses care for patients expecting to recover, *hospice nurses* care for people who are in the final stages of a terminal illness. Typically, a hospice patient has less than six months to live. Hospice nurses provide medical and emotional support to the patients and their families and friends. Hospice care usually takes place in the patient's home, but patients may also receive hospice care in a hospital room, nursing home, or a relative's home.

Medications nurses have additional pharmacology training. They have an extensive knowledge of drugs and their effects on the elderly, and oversee the administration of medications to patients. Many state and federal laws now dictate how facilities can restrain their patients either physically or medicinally, so the medications nurse must be aware of these laws and see that the facility abides by these rules.

Another type of geriatric nurse is a *charge nurse*, who oversees a particular shift of nurses and aides who care for the elderly. Although all health providers are required to do a lot of paperwork to document the care they provide and patients' progress, the charge nurse and administrators are responsible for even more documentation required by HMOs, the federal government, and insurance providers.

Gerontological nurse practitioners are registered nurses who have advanced training and education. This training enables them to carry out many of the responsibilities traditionally handled by physicians. Gerontological nurse practitioners are often based in nursing homes and work with older adults.

Gerontological clinical nurse specialists conduct health assessments and evaluations of elderly patients based on their history, laboratory tests, and their own personal examinations. Following such assessments they arrive at a diagnosis of the patient's problem and deliver care and develop quality-control methods to help correct the patient's medical problem.

Advancement into administration positions such as nursing home administrator or director of nursing is common for persons involved in a geriatric nursing career.

REQUIREMENTS

High School

If you are interested in a geriatric nursing career, be prepared to continue your education after high school. You should take a general college preparatory curriculum, which will include studies in history, social sciences, science, math, English, and computer science. Science and math classes, such as biology, chemistry, physics, algebra, and geometry, will be particularly important to take. Taking four years of English classes is also recommended because these classes will enhance your ability to research, write, and speak effectively. In addition, you should consider taking a foreign language, which will further broaden your communication skills.

Postsecondary Training

To work as a geriatric nurse, you must first become a registered nurse (RN). There are three basic kinds of training programs that you can choose from to become an RN: associate's degree programs, diploma programs, and bachelor's degree programs. The associate in arts in nursing is awarded after completion of a two-year program, which is usually offered by junior or community colleges. You receive hospital training at cooperating hospitals in the general vicinity of the community college. The diploma program, which usually lasts three years, is conducted by hospitals and independent schools.

Perhaps the best route, however, is the bachelor's degree program. One reason is that you will have more time to study a variety of topics in a four-year bachelor's program. As the need for geriatric nurses has grown, more and more bachelor's programs have begun to incorporate classes on gerontological nursing or care of older adults into their core curriculums. This degree will also provide the most career mobility, because a bachelor's degree is required for most supervisory or administrative positions, for jobs in public health agencies, and for admission to graduate nursing programs. The bachelor of science (BS) in nursing is offered by colleges and universities and takes four (in some cases, five) years to complete. Besides taking courses to fulfill your college's general requirements, typical courses you may encounter in a BS nursing program include health assessment, pharmacology, nursing care of adults, health policy and issues, gerontological nursing, and management strategies. Once you have completed any one of these three programs, you must take and pass a licensing examination that is required in all states to become an RN.

To become a gerontological nurse, you'll need to gain experience working in gerontology, and, if you fulfill other requirements, you can become certified as a gerontological nurse by the American Nurses Credentialing Center (ANCC). If you would like to advance into a specialty position, a position with more responsibilities, or a position teaching at a college or university, you will need to pursue additional education. With a master's degree, you can work as a gerontological nurse practitioner or a clinical specialist in gerontological nursing. Nurses in these advanced positions are able to diagnose and treat common illnesses. In addition, they can have prescriptive authority; that is, they can write prescriptions for their patients. Nurses wanting to pursue research need to complete a doctorate degree. The National League for Nursing Accrediting Commission is responsible for accrediting all types of nursing programs offering a certificate, diploma, undergraduate, or graduate degree. The Commission on Collegiate Nursing Education, part of the American Association of Colleges of Nursing, also accredits nursing programs. Both groups provide information on these approved programs.

Certification or Licensing

Certification is available from the ANCC and is highly recommended. Candidates with current RN licenses and a certain amount of experience in the area of practice (gerontology) are eligible to take the specialty and informatics exam. Nurse practitioners and clinical nurse specialists who fulfill certain eligibility requirements and pass an exam can become board certified as advanced practice registered nurses.

All nurses must be licensed to work in the state in which they are employed. They must graduate from an accredited nursing program and pass a national licensing examination to obtain this license. Nurses who wish to specialize in hospice or home health care may choose to attend graduate school.

Other Requirements

Geriatric nurses should enjoy working with and being around older people. They must have a general interest in aging and understand the problems related to growing older. Geriatric nurses must have the ability to get along with the patient's family members and must be able to work well with other professionals such as hospice nurses, chaplains, and social workers. Being able to work as part of a team is essential since many people may become involved in the health care and health needs of the elderly person. Communication skills are also essential. The nurse must be able to communicate with the family and the patient and explain medical terminology and procedures to them so they understand what is being done and why.

EXPLORING

You can explore your interest in nursing and in working with older people in a number of ways. Read books and visit Web sites that deal with the nursing profession. Ask your high school counselor to help you arrange for an information interview with a local nurse. Your school nurse is also someone to consult about the profession and the education required for it. Many hospitals have volunteer programs that provide the opportunity to work during the summer or on a part-time basis, escorting patients to tests, delivering flowers to patients' rooms, and doing other helpful tasks. Volunteering at a hospital will give you a lot of insight as to how hospitals work and how well you like this environment.

To explore how much you enjoy working with older people, volunteer at a senior center, where you may be able to sit in on a card game or teach a crafts project. Volunteer positions as well as part-time or summer jobs also may be available at a nursing home in your area. Use any opportunity you can to visit with older people in your community. You will learn a lot from being around them, and they may be just as eager to learn something from you.

EMPLOYERS

Geriatric nurses work in a variety of settings, depending on their education and personal goals. Many geriatric nurses work in nursing homes, hospitals, retirement communities, or clinics. They may also work in hospice and home care or community nursing programs;

others work in private offices for gerontologists or at government agencies. Nurses who teach or do research are most often in academic settings, usually in buildings that are well lighted, comfortable, and busy.

STARTING OUT

Once you have become a registered nurse, you can apply directly to hospitals, nursing homes, government agencies, and other organizations that hire nurses and offer opportunities to work with older patients. In addition, your school's career services office should have information on job openings. Nurses' associations and their Web sites, professional journals, and newspapers also frequently advertise open positions.

ADVANCEMENT

Advancement in this field often comes with further education. Those with bachelor's degrees can obtain graduate degrees and work as gerontological nurse practitioners or clinical specialists in gerontological nursing. These nurses have greater responsibilities and command higher salaries. Other specialties, such as medications nurse and charge nurse, also require advanced education. Nurses who obtain additional education in administration and management may move into administration positions at nursing departments, hospitals, or nursing homes.

EARNINGS

According to the U.S. Department of Labor (DOL), registered nurses earned a median annual salary of $63,750 in 2009. The lowest paid 10 percent earned less than $43,970, while the middle 50 percent earned between $52,520 and $77,970. The top paid 10 percent made more than $93,700 a year. Registered nurses employed in home health care settings earned mean annual salaries of $63,300, and those who worked at nursing care facilities earned $59,320. Registered nurses who worked in hospice settings earned hourly salaries that ranged from $24.23 to $28.50 in 2008–09, according to the Hospital and Healthcare Compensation Service and the Hospice Association of America. Licensed practical nurses earned between $16.83 and $20.76. Nurse practitioners and clinical nurse specialists typically earn higher salaries.

Salary is determined by many factors, including nursing specialty, education, and place of employment, shift worked, geographical location, and work experience. Flexible schedules and part-time employment opportunities are available for most nurses. Employers usually provide health and life insurance, and some offer educational reimbursements and year-end bonuses to their full-time staff.

WORK ENVIRONMENT

Geriatric nurses can expect to work in a variety of settings depending on their nursing responsibilities. Many geriatric nurses work in nursing homes, hospitals, retirement communities, or in clinics. They may also work with hospice and community nursing programs, or as office nurses for gerontologists.

Although most health care environments will be clean and well lighted there may be some nursing situations where the surroundings may be less than desirable. Some nurses are on call 24 hours a day and may be required to travel to homes in all neighborhoods of a city or in remote rural areas day and night. Safety may be an issue at times.

All nursing careers have some health and disease risks; however, adherence to health and safety guidelines greatly minimizes the chance of contracting infectious diseases such as hepatitis and AIDS. Medical knowledge and good safety measures are also needed to limit the nurse's exposure to toxic chemicals, radiation, and other hazards.

OUTLOOK

Nursing specialties will be in great demand in the future. The DOL predicts that the number of new jobs for registered nurses will be among the largest for any occupation. Most of these jobs will result from current nurses reaching retirement age, in addition to the many technological advances in medicine that will create a need for more people to administer patient care.

Job opportunities for individuals who enter geriatric nursing are predicted to grow at a rate that is much faster than the average for all careers. The Administration on Aging estimates that the number of individuals aged 65 or older will double by 2030. As the older population increases, their need for medical care will also increase. In addition, a 2001 report by the Nursing Institute at the University of Illinois predicts that the ratio of caregivers to the elderly population will decrease by 40 percent between 2010 and 2030. As a result, employment prospects for qualified geriatric nurses are nearly limitless.

FOR MORE INFORMATION

For information on education and scholarships, as well as an overview of expected competencies for geriatric nurses, visit the association's Web site.
American Association of Colleges of Nursing
One Dupont Circle, NW, Suite 530
Washington, DC 20036-1135
Tel: 202-463-6930
http://www.aacn.nche.edu

For information about critical care nursing, contact
American Association of Critical-Care Nurses
101 Columbia
Aliso Viejo, CA 92656-4109
Tel: 800-899-2226
E-mail: info@aacn.org
http://www.aacn.org

To read profiles of geriatric care professionals, visit the society's Web site.
American Geriatrics Society
350 Fifth Avenue, Suite 801
New York, NY 10118-0801
Tel: 212-308-1414
E-mail: info@americangeriatrics.org
http://www.americangeriatrics.org

For information on certification, contact
American Nurses Credentialing Center
8515 Georgia Avenue, Suite 400
Silver Spring, MD 20910-3492
Tel: 800-284-2378
http://www.nursecredentialing.org

For information on careers in aging, visit the association's Web site.
Association for Gerontology in Higher Education
1220 L Street, NW, Suite 901
Washington, DC 20005-4018
Tel: 202-289-9806
E-mail: aghe@aghe.org
http://www.aghe.org

For information about advanced practice gerontological nursing, contact

Gerontological Advanced Practice Nurses Association
East Holly Avenue, Box 56
Pitman, NJ 08071-0056
Tel: 866-355-1392
E-mail: GAPNA@ajj.com
https://www.gapna.org

For general information about hospice care, contact
National Association for Home Care and Hospice
228 Seventh Street, SE
Washington, DC 20003-4306
Tel: 202-547-7424
http://www.nahc.org

For information about a career as a clinical nurse specialist, contact
National Association of Clinical Nurse Specialists
100 North 20th Street, 4th Floor
Philadelphia, PA 19103-1462
Tel: 215-320-3881
http://www.nacns.org

For information about geriatric nursing, contact
National Gerontological Nursing Association
1020 Monarch Street
Lexington, KY 40513-1498
Tel: 800-723-0560
http://www.ngna.org

For industry statistics, contact
National Hospice and Palliative Care Organization
1731 King Street, Suite 100
Alexandria, VA 22314-2720
Tel: 703-837-1500
E-mail: nhpco_info@nhpco.org
http://www.nhpco.org

For career information, contact
Visiting Nurse Associations of America
900 19th Street, NW, Suite 200
Washington, DC 20006-2122

Tel: 202-384-1420
E-mail: vnaa@vnaa.org
http://vnaa.org

INTERVIEW

Susan L. Carlson, MSN, APRN, ACNS-BC, GNP-BC, is a geronto-logical nurse practitioner in the Neurology Department at Audie L. Murphy Veterans Administration Hospital in San Antonio, Texas. She is also the president of the National Gerontological Nursing Association. Susan discussed her career with the editors of Careers in Focus: Nursing.

Q. What made you want to enter this career?

A. Nursing became my first choice for a career when I was in the 10th grade and began to look at options for lifelong work. I enjoyed both science and business but after taking biology, I became fascinated by the human body and how each system worked together. I developed an early appreciation for how older adults adapted to and enjoyed life, despite having serious health problems. Nursing was then a natural choice—no other career would have satisfied my desire for the intense personal connection I have with my patients and the challenges of applying the science to my work.

Q. Can you please describe a day in your life on the job?

A. My work as a nurse practitioner is diverse because I see patients in an outpatient clinic three days a week, the traditional role of a nurse practitioner, but I'm also a certified clinical nurse specialist and help manage and monitor a large pool of neurology patients who are seen by other doctors and providers. During my clinic days, I complete history and physicals on patients who have a number of neurological disorders—seizures, multiple sclerosis, Parkinson's disease, strokes, and other problems such as headaches. Along with the patient and family, we develop a treatment plan that typically includes medication management, health maintenance and education, and appropriate follow up with their primary care provider. Helping the patient understand and navigate a big health care system like the Veterans Health Care System is an important part of my work. Patients and their families are very appreciative for the guidance and understanding provided by nurses, and it is very satisfying for me as well.

Q. What are some of the pros and cons of your job?

A. The best part of my work is the interaction with the patients and having the knowledge and skills that really make a difference in their lives. Nurses are prepared to assess the whole person—their physical, psychosocial, and emotional needs. For me, the holistic approach is one of the greatest benefits of the being a nurse. Of course, the extensive paperwork required to document in the medical record and all of the other associated forms can be overwhelming. The tremendous responsibility of caring for patients is stressful at times, especially when they have multiple medical and social problems that all need to be addressed. Thankfully, nurses work with other professionals on the team, and it is important to remember that we can't do it alone.

Q. What are the most important personal and professional qualities for people in your career?

A. Be committed to a life of learning. Of course, that is important for any profession. However, the speed at which health information changes is incredibly fast. Being naturally curious and self-directed are also desired qualities. Being a good listener with keen observational skills are the hallmarks of a great nurse. Add a good sense of humor to the mix and a long-satisfying career in nursing awaits you!

Q. What advice would you give to young people who are interested in the field?

A. My advice to anyone considering a career in nursing is to look for opportunities to volunteer or work in a health care setting to gain real-life experience. Don't accept the portrayal of nursing in the media as truth. Interview nurses who work in various settings. Ask if your local hospital has a "shadow" program that allows young people to spend a day or two alongside a practicing nurse. Write down your reasons on why you think you'd enjoy being a nurse and see if, after several months of "investigational work," you still agree with your reasons. Keeping a journal is an excellent way to capture your thoughts and feelings.

Q. **What is the employment outlook for gerontological nurse practitioners?**

A. Given the large number of older adults living into their 80s and 90s, the need for advance practice nurses prepared to care for their health needs will continue to grow. I predict there will be employment opportunities created by the greater demands and expectations of the "boomers" who will help shape the future of health care in the coming decades.

Health Advocates

OVERVIEW

Health advocates, also known as *patient representatives* and *patient advocates*, work with and on behalf of patients to resolve issues ranging from getting insurance coverage to dealing with complaints about the medical staff to explaining a doctor's treatment plan. In addition to patients, health advocates often interact with physicians, hospitals, health maintenance organizations, insurance companies, and government agencies, to name a few. Advocates are employed by hospitals, nonprofit groups, and other health facilities, such as nursing homes. They also may work as independent contractors.

HISTORY

The world of health care has grown increasingly complex. New scientific discoveries allow doctors to better understand diseases and technology advancements that lead to new and better ways to treat patients. At the same time, government regulations, insurance company policies, hospital rules, and the legal field have all combined to make getting the appropriate health care a complicated process. It can sometimes seem as if the interests of patients get lost in the shuffle. It can be difficult for even the most informed patients to make sure they are getting the most beneficial treatment. This situation has led to the need for someone to work on behalf of patients, promoting their interests everywhere from the doctor's office to the Senate floor.

Although advocates for patients have existed for many years (some cite Florence Nightingale as the first advocate), the recognized

Nontraditional Nursing Specialty: Transcultural Nursing

Transcultural nursing focuses on the cultural beliefs, values, and practices of people to help them maintain and regain their health, or face death in meaningful ways. Nurses in this specialty try to understand cultures and their specific care needs and how to provide care that fits their ways rather than automatically imposing traditional Western medical practices on them. They provide culturally congruent care for well, sick, disabled, or dying patients of Mexican, Vietnamese, Japanese, African, Anglo, and other cultures and subcultures.

profession of health advocate did not really begin to develop until the late 20th century. One step in this development was the acknowledgement by professionals that patients had rights and deserved quality treatment. An example of this occurred in 1973 when the American Hospital Association, a national organization representing hospitals, health care networks, and patients, adopted its first version of a Patient's Bill of Rights. Among other things, the bill recognizes that patients have the right to respectful care, the right to receive understandable information about their treatment, and the right to make their own decisions. Although the profession of health advocates was fairly small in the 1970s, its popularity has increased steadily since then, and health advocates have become important members of the health care community.

THE JOB

As insurance companies, doctors, and even the U.S. government do battle over the health care system, it can sometimes seem as if the interests of patients are being overlooked.

Because the world of health care has become so complex in recent years, it's difficult for even the most informed patients to make sure changes in the system will benefit them. Health advocates enter this struggle on the patients' behalf, using their own health care expertise to promote the interests of patients in the private and public sectors.

Primarily, there are three types of health care advocates. Those that are employed by large companies such as hospitals, insurance companies, large physician groups, and other health organizations are often called *patient representatives*, or *consumer health advocates.* The second category of health advocates works primarily for nonprofit organizations that deal with a wide variety of medical and insurance concerns, or they might work for a group that targets a particular illness or disease, such as cancer or lupus. The third group of health advocates works for private advocacy firms.

Many hospitals have seen the need and benefits of having a team devoted to resolving complaints of patients and their families and watching out for the interests of the patients as well as of the hospital. Patient representatives receive complaints from the patient or the family and work toward a resolution to the problem. The problem may range from issues between two patients sharing a room, to miscommunication between the patient and medical staff, to misplaced personal items. For example, if a patient felt mistreated by a hospital staff member, the patient representative must hear both sides of the case, determine if the claim is valid or a misunderstanding, and hopefully work out a peaceful and satisfactory resolution.

Patient representatives also document patients' concerns and experience with the hospital and its staff. Complaints and the method of resolution are recorded to help in future cases. Measuring and recording patient satisfaction are important because the hospital uses this information in finding areas to improve. Another important role of representatives is to interpret medical procedures or unfamiliar medical terms and to answer patients' questions in regards to hospital procedures or health insurance concerns. They also educate patients, as well as the hospital staff, about the patient's bill of rights, advance directives, and issues of bioethics. Sometimes they handle special religious or dietary needs of the patient or personal requests, such as commemorating a birthday.

While patient representatives work for the patient's well-being as well as their employer's best interests, health advocates employed by nonprofits act as the patient's champion against insurance companies, employers, and creditors. Many times patients are denied much-needed medical treatments because insurance companies consider them to be experimental. Certain drugs might be denied because of the way they are taken. Health advocates provide assistance in getting these issues resolved. They help identify the type of health insurance and the depth of coverage the patient has and organize paperwork and referrals from physicians and hospitals. Sometimes patients also need help composing letters to insurance companies explaining their situation. Health advocates also make phone calls to physicians and insurance companies on behalf of the patient.

Patients sometimes encounter job discrimination because of existing illnesses or extended medical leaves, and this is another area in which health advocates can help. Many nonprofit groups also have lawyers on staff that provide legal counsel. Also, with any serious illness, financial concerns are likely. Health advocates can offer suggestions on how to get the most from a patient's insurance coverage, negotiate with physicians and hospitals to lower costs, and work with pharmaceutical companies in providing expensive medications at a lower cost.

Health advocates may choose to work independent of a hospital, group, or organization. Such advocates act as consultants and may have their own private practice or work for an advocacy firm. Their cases usually involve patients with a variety of issues and concerns. They usually charge a flat fee per case.

REQUIREMENTS

High School

If you are interested in working as a health advocate, take a broad range of classes in high school. Advocates need an extensive base of knowledge that covers medical, financial, emotional, and legal areas. Courses that are especially useful include business, mathematics, biology, health, and chemistry. Be sure to take four years of English as well as speech classes, because health advocates need strong oral and written communication skills. Learning a foreign language, such as Spanish, will also be useful. You may also want to take government, psychology, and computer science classes to prepare for this career.

Postsecondary Training

There is no single educational route to take to become a health advocate; the backgrounds that health advocates bring to the field tend to be as varied as their places of employment. Nevertheless, a knowledge of health care systems and medical terminology are important for you to have. Most employers prefer that you have at least a bachelor's degree. Some students choose to get degrees in health administration, premed, biology, or nursing. Helpful courses to take include communications, management, conflict resolution, and medical terminology. Some schools also offer classes in patient representation. As this profession has become more popular, schools are beginning to offer specialized programs of study. Sarah Lawrence College, for example, offers a master's degree in health advocacy. Course work for this degree includes nature of illness, position of the health advocate, health law, and ethics, as well as fieldwork.

Other Requirements

Advocates seem to agree that the most important training advocates can bring to this field is a sincere desire to work for the health and well-being of others. You can develop this commitment through community service, volunteer positions at hospitals, or caring for a loved one who has a serious illness. Though knowledge of the health care system is important, you can't do your job as an advocate unless you have the skills to convey that information in a convincing way to your audience, whether that audience is a medical ethics board or an insurance company clerk. Health advocates must be persistent and have strong problem-solving skills. Advocates must combine their medical and health administration expertise in creative ways, devising new negotiation strategies all the time. Often, obtaining the best possible outcome for patients means developing a specific plan for each new situation. Other important skills are the ability to communicate well and think analytically.

EXPLORING

One way to explore this field is by talking to people in it. Ask your school counselor to help you set up an information interview with a health advocate in your area. You may also be able to arrange to spend part of a day shadowing the advocate. Another way to learn more about this field is to learn about the issues that relate to patient advocacy. Visit your local library or surf the Internet to learn more. A good way to find out whether this field is for you is by volunteering at an organization that helps people. You might consider joining a religious group that helps the elderly or volunteering at a local hospital. Hospitals and nursing homes may also have paid part-time or summer positions available. Taking such a job will give you experience working in a health care environment and the opportunity to learn about patients' day-to-day needs. Stay up to date in this field by visiting related Web sites, such as Healthfinder.gov (http://www .healthfinder.gov).

EMPLOYERS

In addition to nonprofit organizations, private firms that specialize in patient advocacy have begun to spring up around the country. Some hospitals, specialty practices, and managed care organizations now hire patient representatives to deal with patients' complaints, and corporations supporting large health care plans for their employees have begun to do the same. Advocates working on more widespread issues in the health care industry often find employment at government agencies, community organizations, and schools developing health advocacy courses or programs.

Job descriptions for advocates may also vary significantly, depending on your place of employment. Patient representatives employed by hospitals, doctors' groups, or large corporations still work for improved health care for patients, but also they must balance their employers' interests with those of patients. For that reason, advocates at work on the insurance or treatment side of the industry may find that their jobs resemble more typical customer service positions designed to receive and resolve consumer complaints. Advocates employed by nonprofits don't have the same responsibility to consider the financial needs of the doctors and insurance companies, and they may consequently have more freedom.

STARTING OUT

Contact your college's career services office for help in finding your first job. Some hospitals advertise job openings for health advocates in the classified section of the newspaper. You may have to start out in another position in a hospital and move into health advocacy once you've gained some experience.

ADVANCEMENT

Health advocates who work as members of a staff in a hospital can advance to department manager or other administrative positions. Some health advocates may find jobs in hospices, in AIDS programs, or with the U.S. Department of Health and Human Services.

EARNINGS

Although independent patient advocates may have more opportunities to put the patient first, they sometimes gain that freedom at the expense of job stability and a predictable salary. Patient representatives employed by hospitals, doctors' groups, and corporations can expect to earn a regular salary of $45,000 to $110,000 a year. A self-employed patient advocate or an advocate at a private firm will likely work for consultant fees that tend to vary from job to job. Some independent patient advocates charge flat fees from $75 to $150 to analyze insurance statements; if the advocate identifies any savings for the client, the advocate and client split the savings 50–50. While these rates may work out to significant earnings per year, independent advocates have no guaranteed business, and a slow year will mean a lower income. At nonprofit organizations, advocates can rely on predictable salaries; however, because nonprofits often lack the financial wherewithal of hospitals and corporations, advocates working at nonprofits tend to earn salaries at the lower end of the pay scale.

Health advocates usually receive benefits such as vacation days, sick leave, health and life insurance, and a savings and pension program.

WORK ENVIRONMENT

The type of employment that an advocate pursues largely determines their work environment. High-profile advocates striving to improve patient conditions on a national level may travel frequently, deliver speeches and seminars, and even lunch with members of Congress. Patient representatives at hospitals or managed care organizations experience a different work environment: a more standard business atmosphere, with little travel outside of the office. While it's not typical, some advocates at nonprofit or small community groups work from home. Any health advocate, though, can expect busy and varied workdays; interaction with many people is part of this job.

OUTLOOK

According to the U.S. Department of Labor (DOL), employment in the health services industry will increase as the population ages and new medical technologies evolve. In fact, the DOL expects the number of jobs will increase by 22 percent between 2008 and 2018. While this figure includes all areas of health services, growth in health services is likely to contribute to health advocacy employment in the long run. As the number of patients increases and the field of health services becomes larger and more complex, patients' need for advocates can be expected to increase as well.

As the field of health advocacy grows, it most likely will become more established. New graduate programs can be expected to develop, and eventually undergraduate programs may exist as well. While the wide range of jobs available means that the field should stay diverse and deregulated, certain areas of health advocacy may develop certification procedures for their subgroups over the next five years.

FOR MORE INFORMATION

For information about education programs and to read selected articles from the Journal of the Health Advocacy Program, *contact*

Health Advocacy Program
Sarah Lawrence College
1 Mead Way
Bronxville, NY 10708-5940
Tel: 914-337-0700
E-mail: grad@sarahlawrence.edu
http://www.slc.edu/graduate/programs/health_advocacy/index
    .html

For general information about health advocacy careers, contact

Society for Healthcare Consumer Advocacy
American Hospital Association
155 North Wacker Drive, Suite 400
Chicago, IL 60606-1727
Tel: 312-422-3700
http://www.shca-aha.org

Home Health Care and Hospice Nurses

OVERVIEW

Home health care nurses, also called *visiting nurses*, provide home-based health care under the direction of a physician. They care for persons who may be recovering from an accident, illness, surgery, cancer, or childbirth. They may work for a community organization, a private health care provider, or they may be independent nurses who work on a contract basis.

While home health care nurses care for patients expecting to recover, *hospice nurses* care for people who are in the final stages of a terminal illness. Typically, a hospice patient has less than six months to live. Hospice nurses provide medical and emotional support to the patients and their families and friends. Hospice care usually takes place in the patient's home, but patients may also receive hospice care in a hospital room, nursing home, or a relative's home. The National Hospice and Palliative Care Organization (NHPCO) states, "Hospice care professionals and volunteers provide services that address all of the symptoms of a terminal illness—ranging from physical to emotional to spiritual—with the aim of promoting comfort and dignity and living as fully as possible at life's end."

Both home health care and hospice nursing professions practice a team approach in caring for their patients. Support people, such as volunteers, aides, therapists, social workers, and clergy, are often involved in the patient's care, as well as doctors.

QUICK FACTS

School Subjects
Biology
Chemistry

Personal Skills
Helping/teaching
Technical/scientific

Work Environment
Primarily indoors
Primarily multiple locations

Minimum Education Level
Some postsecondary training

Salary Range
$43,970 to $63,300 to $93,700+

Certification or Licensing
Recommended (certification)
Required by all states (licensing)

Outlook
Much faster than the average

DOT
079

GOE
14.02.01

NOC
3152

O*NET
29-1111.00

HISTORY

Home health care originated with the visiting nurse agencies more than 120 years ago. At that time, the need was critical; there were few hospitals to serve many communities, and where they existed, they usually cared only for those who were seriously ill. Patients were cared for by their families at home. The introduction of trained medical professionals into the household not only improved the quality of medical care available, but brought compassion and support to help both the patient and the family.

Though they were originally intended to serve communities without adequate health care, home health care and hospice nurses are now in demand for another reason. Today, as patients spend less time in the hospital and as more medical procedures are done on an outpatient basis, the need for professional follow-up care in the home is essential. Recovery, rehabilitation, and care for illnesses and injuries are happening in the home. Approximately 12 million people received home care in 2009, according to the National Association for Home Care and Hospice.

THE JOB

Home health care nurses are often assigned to patients after the patients are discharged from a hospital or after they have had outpatient procedures. They provide follow-up health care on a regular basis and establish a one-on-one patient-nurse relationship. Some home health care nurses also work with patients who have acute, ongoing illnesses such as diabetes or high blood pressure.

According to Joan Bissing, RN, BS, a hospice nurse in California, "[Home health care nurses and hospice nurses] often provide wound care, draw blood, and give medications. We may also do chemotherapy, or IV therapy."

"It is essential that a hospice or home health care nurse have nursing experience before going into this specialty," Bissing states. "While most nurses work directly under a doctor, hospice and home health care nurses must have a specialty in high-tech nursing and a knowledge of different diseases since they are often required to work independently."

Although they need to be able to work alone, nurses in this specialty must also know how to work as a member of a team. A variety of hospice personnel, such as doctors, social workers, chaplains, volunteers, counselors, and aides, become involved with the patient as the illness progresses. Home health care and hospice nurses work with all aspects and ages of the population. Their duties vary greatly depending on their patients, their illnesses, and the care or support they need.

Sometimes the job requires the nurse to "just listen," says Bissing. "We can sometimes sense that our terminally ill patient is unsettled about something, such as past relationships, and then we need to be proactive and get the proper counseling or clergy to help the patient deal with the problem and find peace."

The hospice nurse is often a source of comfort to the patient and his or her family and friends. "Some patients may say, 'I've had enough treatments. I just want to live my final days as peacefully and pain free as possible,'" Bissing says. The hospice nurse must work with the hospice team to make sure those wishes are carried out. "At that point, we focus on giving the patient the best quality of life we can, keeping the patient as comfortable and pain free as possible."

There are rewards to every member of the hospice team, according to Bissing. "They all learn something from each of their patients. Sometimes it is an experience they won't ever forget." She goes on, "It can be as simple as a touch of the hand with a difficult patient, or as complex as facilitating a reunion with a long-lost relative before the patient's death."

One thing Bissing wants anyone thinking of going into this profession to remember, "Never forget that it's okay to cry. Shared tears are often part of the patient care."

As with almost all health care professions today, nurses spend a great deal of time keeping records and charts and documenting the services they provide in order to meet insurance, government, and Medicare requirements.

REQUIREMENTS

High School

If you are interested in becoming a nurse, you should take mathematics and science courses, including biology, chemistry, and physics. Health courses will also be helpful. English and speech courses will help you develop basic communication skills that you will use with patients and coworkers.

Postsecondary Training

Nurses who specialize in a specific nursing field such as home health care or hospice nursing must first become registered nurses. (See the article "Registered Nurses.") Many home health care and hospice nurses are required to have some nursing experience, preferably in acute care, because they are required to work with patients with a wide range of health problems. Entry-level requirements depend on the home health care agency, the hospice organization, and the availability of nurses in that specialty and geographical region. Nurses who wish to specialize in hospice or home health care may choose to attend graduate school.

Certification or Licensing
Certification is a voluntary process. It is offered by the American Nurses Credentialing Center and other nursing organizations.

All states and the District of Columbia require a license to practice nursing. To obtain a license, graduates of approved nursing schools must pass a national examination. Nurses may be licensed by more than one state. In some states, continuing education is a condition for license renewal. Different titles require different education and training levels.

Other Requirements
Home health care and hospice nurses should feel comfortable working with patients of all ages and people from all cultural backgrounds. Good communication skills are essential, including the ability to listen and respond to the patients' needs. Home health care and hospice nurses must be able to work independently, have good organizational skills, and also have the ability to supervise aides and other support people. Flexibility is also a requirement because duties vary greatly from hour to hour and day to day. Many hospice nurses are on call and their work is mentally stressful. "There is a lot of burnout in hospice nursing," confirms Joan Bissing. "Hospice nurses usually don't stay in the field long. It is hard work and very intense. Much of hospice nursing is treating the symptoms of the disease, rather than curing the disease."

EXPLORING
There are many ways to explore the field of nursing while in high school. Check out your school or local library to read books on nursing careers. You can also arrange to talk with your high school counselor, school nurse, and even local public health nurses. Consider visiting a hospital to observe nurses at work and to talk with personnel. You may be able to work as a volunteer. Other volunteer work experiences may be found with the Red Cross or community health services.

To explore the career of home health care and hospice nursing, try contacting local agencies and programs that provide home care services and request information on employment guidelines or training programs. Home health organizations may sponsor open houses to enlighten the community to the services they provide. This could allow you to meet the staff involved in hiring and program development and to learn about job opportunities. Finally, ask if it may be possible to accompany a home health care or hospice nurse on a home visit.

EMPLOYERS

According to the National Association for Home Care and Hospice, there are more than 17,000 home health care agencies in the United States. There are more than 3,250 hospice programs in the United States, according to the NHPCO. These health care providers often have training programs for prospective employees. Home health and hospice nurses might also find employment with hospitals that operate their own community outreach programs. Most hospitals, however, hire through agencies.

STARTING OUT

Home care and hospice nurses must first become registered nurses by completing an educational program and passing the licensing examination. Once registered, nurses may apply for employment directly to hospitals, nursing homes, companies, and government agencies that hire nurses. Home care and hospice jobs can also be obtained through school career services offices, employment agencies specializing in placement of nursing personnel, or state employment offices. Other sources of jobs include nurses' associations, professional journals, Web sites, and newspaper want ads.

For a list of employment prospects, check the local Yellow Pages for agencies that provide health care to the aged and disabled or family service. Many agencies or nursing care facilities offer free training to qualified employees.

ADVANCEMENT

Additional experience and education often bring higher pay and increased responsibility. Home health care and hospice nurses may advance to management or supervisory positions. Those who would rather continue to work with clients may branch into more specialized care or a related field and pursue additional training. Other possible fields include social work, physical or occupational therapy, and dietetics.

EARNINGS

According to the U.S. Department of Labor (DOL), median annual earnings of registered nurses who worked in home health care services were $63,300 in 2009. Salaries for all registered nurses ranged from less than $43,970 to more than $93,700.

According to the National Association for Home Care and Hospice, in 2009 registered nurses earned hourly wages that ranged from $25.64 to $31.09 (or from about $53,330 to $64,670 annually). Licensed practical nurse earned from $17.97 to $22.47 (or from approximately $37,380 to $46,738 annually).

Salary is determined by many factors, including nursing specialty, education, place of employment, geographical location, and work experience. Flexible schedules are available for most full-time nurses, and part-time work is often available. Employers usually provide health and life insurance, and some offer educational reimbursements and year-end bonuses to their full-time staff.

WORK ENVIRONMENT

Most hospice and home health care nurses care for their patients in the patients' homes, nursing homes, or in the homes of their caregivers, so the work environment can be as varied as their patients' lifestyles. In addition, patients and family members can be very tense during this stressful period of their lives and they may be unpleasant and uncooperative at times. Some nurses are on call 24 hours a day and may be required to travel to homes in all neighborhoods of a city or in remote rural areas day and night. Safety may be an issue at times.

All nursing careers have some health and disease risks; however, adherence to health and safety guidelines greatly minimizes the chance of contracting infectious diseases such as hepatitis and AIDS. Medical knowledge and good safety measures are also needed to limit the nurse's exposure to toxic chemicals, radiation, and other hazards.

OUTLOOK

Nursing specialties will be in great demand in the future. From 2008 to 2018, employment for registered nurses who work in home health care services is expected to increase by 33 percent, according to the DOL. Part-time job opportunities are also plentiful in the nursing profession.

The nursing demand will be felt particularly in the hospice and home health care fields. The U.S. Bureau of the Census estimates that the number of individuals aged 65 or older will double by 2050. As the older population increases, their need for medical care will also increase. Hospice participation has grown at a dramatic rate, especially among those involved with Medicare. This number is expected to increase as the population ages and health care costs rise.

FOR MORE INFORMATION

For information on education and scholarships, visit the AACN Web site.

American Association of Colleges of Nursing (AACN)
One Dupont Circle, NW, Suite 530
Washington, DC 20036-1135
Tel: 202-463-6930
http://www.aacn.nche.edu

For information on certification, contact
American Nurses Credentialing Center
8515 Georgia Avenue, Suite 400
Silver Spring, MD 20910-3492
Tel: 800-284-2378
http://www.nursecredentialing.org

For information on hospice care, contact
Hospice Education Institute
3 Unity Square
PO Box 98
Machiasport, MA 04655-0098
Tel: 800-331-1620
E-mail: info@hospiceworld.org
http://www.hospiceworld.org

For general information about hospice care, contact
National Association for Home Care and Hospice
228 Seventh Street, SE
Washington, DC 20003-4306
Tel: 202-547-7424
http://www.nahc.org

For information about geriatric nursing, contact
National Gerontological Nursing Association
1020 Monarch Street, Suite 300 B
Lexington, KY 40513-1868
Tel: 800-723-0560
http://www.ngna.org

For industry statistics, contact
National Hospice and Palliative Care Organization
1731 King Street, Suite 100
Alexandria, VA 22314-2720
Tel: 703-837-1500
E-mail: nhpco_info@nhpco.org
http://www.nhpco.org

For information on home health care, contact
Visiting Nurse Associations of America
900 19th Street, NW, Suite 200
Washington, DC 20006-2122
Tel: 202-384-1420
E-mail: vnaa@vnaa.org
http://www.vnaa.org

Legal Nurse Consultants

OVERVIEW

Legal nurse consultants are members of a litigation team that deals with medical malpractice, personal injury, and product liability lawsuits as well as other medically related legal cases. They may be employed independently on a contract or retainer basis; or they may be employed by a law firm, insurance company, corporation, government agency, or as part of a risk management department in a hospital. Legal nurse consultants are trained nurses who have a thorough understanding of medical issues and trends. They utilize their clinical experience, knowledge of health care standards, and medical resources to assist litigation teams and act as liaisons between the legal and health care communities. Their primary role is to evaluate, analyze, and render informed opinions regarding health care. They practice in both plaintiff and defense capacities in collaboration with attorneys and others involved in legal processes.

HISTORY

Nurses have served as expert witnesses in nursing malpractice cases for many years. But it was not until the early 1970s, according to the American Association of Legal Nurse Consultants (AALNC), that nurses began to receive compensation for providing this much-needed expertise to the legal community. As nursing and medical malpractice litigation increased in the 1980s, more nurses were needed to serve as expert witnesses in legal proceedings. During

School Subjects
Biology
Chemistry

Personal Skills
Helping/teaching
Technical/scientific

Work Environment
Primarily indoors
Primarily multiple locations

Minimum Education Level
Some postsecondary training

Salary Range
$53,427 to $85,000 to $103,000+

Certification or Licensing
Voluntary (certification)
Required by all states (licensing)

Outlook
Faster than the average

DOT
N/A

GOE
04.02.02, 14.02.01

NOC
3152

O*NET-SOC
29-1111.00

Learn More About It

American Association of Legal Nurse Consultants. *Legal Terminology Primer for the Legal Nurse Consultant.* Chicago: American Association of Legal Nurse Consultants, 2003.

American Nurses Association. *Legal Nurse Consulting: Scope and Standards of Practice.* Silver Spring, Md.: American Nurses Association, 2006.

Blevins, Nancy, Renee Miller, JoAnn Pugh, and Elizabeth Riggs. *Developing an Independent Legal Nurse Consulting Practice.* Chicago: American Association of Legal Nurse Consultants, 2001.

Iyer, Patricia, ed. *Legal Nurse Consulting: Principles & Practice.* 2d ed. Chicago: American Association of Legal Nurse Consultants, 2003.

Peterson, Ann M., and Lynda Kopishke, eds. *Legal Nurse Consulting: Principles and Practice.* 3d ed. Boca Raton, Fla.: CRC Press, 2010.

Weishapple, Cynthia L. *Introduction to Legal Nurse Consulting.* Florence, Ky.: Delmar Cengage Learning, 2000.

this time, according to the AALNC, nurses also began assisting lawyers with understanding medical records and literature, hospital policies and procedures, and medical testimony. Law firms quickly realized that legal nurse consultants were a knowledgeable, cost-effective alternative to physician consultants and began to hire these professionals to assist them with not only nursing and medical malpractice issues, but also personal injury and criminal cases.

The American Association of Legal Nurse Consultants was founded in 1989 to serve the professional needs of legal nurse consultants. It has approximately 52 local chapters nationwide and 3,500 members.

THE JOB

Legal nurse consultants' job responsibilities vary depending on the case and its medical implications. When working on a case, they may conduct client interviews, which involves talking to persons who feel they have a legal claim against a medical facility or doctor or nurse, or as a result of an accident.

They may research past medical cases and treatments. They often advise attorneys regarding medical facts, treatments, and other medical issues that are relevant to a case. Legal nurse consultants obtain and organize medical records, and locate and procure evidence. They may identify, interview, and retain expert witnesses. They may also assist with depositions and trials, including developing and preparing exhibits for jury or judge trials.

As part of legal teams, legal nurse consultants are often required to do considerable research and paperwork. "As a legal nurse consultant," says Sherri Reed, BSN, RN, LNCC, former president of the American Association of Legal Nurse Consultants (AALNC), "you must be totally responsible for your part of the job. If information is to be gathered and reports written, you need to get it done. There is no one to take over at shift change. It is entirely your responsibility and you can't pass it on to someone else."

Independent legal nurse consultants must also be responsible for getting their work done within a strict deadline. They often work under a contract and must produce the records, information, and reports within a specified time frame.

In addition, they must generate their own clients. This requires that they not only be nurses, but be business-minded as well and do their own marketing to the legal field. Independent legal nurse consultants need to learn and practice business skills such as marketing, sales, and record keeping.

"Nurses are nurturers by nature," says Reed. "Because of these predominant traits, many need to learn to be aggressive and assertive and be their own salespeople if they are going to find work."

Legal nurse consultants can expect their jobs to be demanding, but that is what Reed likes best about her job. "I like my independence and using my knowledge to analyze and research cases. It is challenging and stimulating. There are always new cases and issues."

REQUIREMENTS

High School
In high school, take mathematics and science courses, including biology, chemistry, and physics. Health courses will also be helpful. English and speech courses should not be neglected because you must be able to communicate well with lawyers and other legal professionals. Business and accounting classes will provide you with the basic tools necessary to run a business.

Postsecondary Training
Legal nurse consultants must first become registered nurses. "All legal nurse consultants must have clinical nursing experience," says Reed, who is employed as a legal nurse consultant with an Indiana

law firm. "This is extremely important since they need this work experience to draw on in order to present cases and testify. They must have up-to-date medical knowledge they can utilize."

Legal nurse consultants should have work experience in critical care areas such as hospital emergency rooms, intensive care units, and obstetrics, since these are the areas that are most likely to be involved in litigation. Legal education is not a prerequisite, although many legal nurse consultants acquire knowledge of the legal system by consulting with attorneys, taking classes, and attending seminars.

A few colleges (such as Bergen Community College, Elgin Community College, Kent State University, and Madonna University) offer associate degrees and advanced certificates in legal consulting.

Many independent legal nurse consultants are practicing nurses. According to Reed, "It is important for legal nurse consultants to stay abreast of changes in the medical field. They need to actively practice nursing or take continuing education courses to stay current. They must be able to apply their knowledge and evaluate medical issues in litigation."

The AALNC offers an online course for aspiring legal nurse consultants. Visit http://www.aalnc.org/onlinelearning for more information.

Certification or Licensing

The legal nurse consultant certified (LNCC) program is the only certification in legal nurse consulting recognized by the American Association of Legal Nurse Consultants. Administered by the American Legal Nurse Consultant Certification Board, it is the only legal nurse consulting certification approved by the American Board of Nursing Specialties because it meets their stringent criteria. The LNCC program promotes the recognition of experience and knowledge of the legal nurse consulting specialty practice of nursing. The certification, which is voluntary, is renewed every five years through continuing education or reexamination and continued practice in the specialty.

You must pass a licensing exam to become a nurse. Licensing is required in all 50 states, and license renewal or continuing education credits are also required periodically. In some cases, licensing in one state will automatically grant licensing in reciprocal states. For more information, contact your state's nursing board. (See the National Council of State Boards of Nursing Web site at https://www.ncsbn.org for contact information.)

Other Requirements

To be a successful legal nurse consultant, you should enjoy organizing information and writing reports, be able to explain medical issues and procedures to people with nonmedical backgrounds, and be skilled to handle multiple tasks under deadline pressure. You should also have strong reasoning skills, self-motivation, and the ability to work well with many types of people.

If you also practice as a nurse, you should enjoy working with people and be able to give directions as well as follow instructions and work as part of a health care team. Anyone interested in becoming a registered nurse should also have a strong desire to continue learning because new tests, procedures, and technologies are constantly being developed for the medical world.

EXPLORING

You can learn more about nursing and legal issues by visiting the Web sites of nursing and legal associations, reading books or magazines (such as *The Journal of Legal Nurse Consulting*, which is available from the AALNC, http://www.aalnc.org/edupro/journal .cfm) on the subjects, or conducting an information interview with a registered nurse, a legal nurse consultant, or a lawyer who specializes in health care issues. You might also visit hospitals to observe the work and to talk with hospital personnel.

Some hospitals now have extensive volunteer service programs in which students can work after school, on weekends, or during vacations. You can find other volunteer work experiences with the Red Cross or community health services.

To learn more about the legal aspects of legal nurse consulting, you might consider trying to get an internship at a law firm that specializes in health care law.

EMPLOYERS

Legal nurse consultants may be employed independently on a contract or retainer basis, or they may be employed by a law firm, insurance company, corporation, or government agency, or as part of a risk management department in a hospital.

STARTING OUT

The only way to become a registered nurse is through completion of one of the three kinds of educational programs plus passing the licensing examination. Registered nurses may apply for employment directly to hospitals, nursing homes, and companies and government agencies that hire nurses. Jobs can also be obtained through school career services offices, by signing up with employment agencies specializing in placement of nursing personnel, or through state employment offices. Other sources of jobs include nurses' associations, professional journals, and newspaper want ads.

ADVANCEMENT

Administrative and supervisory positions in the nursing field go to nurses who have earned at least the bachelor of science degree in nursing. Nurses with many years of experience who are graduates of the diploma program may achieve supervisory positions, but requirements for such promotions have become more difficult in recent years and in many cases require at least the bachelor of science in nursing degree.

Legal nurse consultants with considerable experience may advance to supervisory positions or move on to open their own consulting companies. Others may choose to earn a law degree and become nurse attorneys.

EARNINGS

Persons who work as independent legal nurse consultants are usually paid on an hourly basis that can range from $125 to $150 per hour. The fee depends on the type of services they are performing, such as testifying, reviewing records, or doing medical research, and also reflects their experience and reputation. In addition, fees vary in different parts of the country. Some legal nurse consultants may work on a retainer basis with one or more clients.

Many legal nurse consultants who work for law firms and other businesses and institutions are employed full or part time. Their salaries vary by experience, geographic location, and areas of expertise. The full-time salary range is from under $53,427 to a small percentage making more than $103,000. According to Allnursing-schools.com, legal nurse consultants with associate's degrees earn median annual salaries of $74,254; those with bachelor's degrees earn median annual salaries of $85,000. Some litigation situations may require that consultants work overtime.

General employment benefits such as health and life insurance, vacation time, and sick leave may be offered to full-time legal nurse consultants.

WORK ENVIRONMENT

Working environments may vary depending on the consultants' responsibilities and their legal cases. According to a survey conducted by AALNC, 53 percent of legal nurse consultants were in independent practice, and law firms employed 32 percent. Office environments where consultants work are usually clean and well lighted. However, research and interview requirements may take consultants to communities that range from safe to less than desirable.

OUTLOOK

Nursing specialties will be in great demand in the future. The U.S. Department of Labor reports that employment for registered nurses is expected to grow much faster than the average for all careers through 2018. As long as there is litigation involving medical issues, one can expect this specialty nursing field to continue to grow.

The outlook for legal nurse consultants is excellent. According to Sherri Reed, "It is an up-and-coming profession. Our association [AALNC] has grown rapidly and we hope to increase the profession's visibility."

FOR MORE INFORMATION

For information on educational opportunities in nursing, contact
American Association of Colleges of Nursing
One Dupont Circle, NW, Suite 530
Washington, DC 20036-1135
Tel: 202-463-6930
http://www.aacn.nche.edu

For information on certification and to read Getting Started in Legal Nurse Consulting: An Introduction to the Specialty, *visit the AALNC Web site.*
American Association of Legal Nurse Consultants (AALNC)
401 North Michigan Avenue
Chicago, IL 60611-4255
Tel: 877-402-2562
E-mail: info@aalnc.org
http://www.aalnc.org

Licensed Practical Nurses

OVERVIEW

Licensed practical nurses (LPNs), a specialty of the nursing profession, are sometimes called *licensed vocational nurses*. LPNs are trained to assist in the care and treatment of patients. They may assist registered nurses and physicians or work under various other circumstances. They perform many of the general duties of nursing and may be responsible for some clerical duties. LPNs work in hospitals, public health agencies, nursing homes, or in home health. Approximately 753,600 licensed practical nurses are employed in the United States.

HISTORY

Until the 1870s, nursing care in the United States was provided by concerned individuals—usually women—who applied their practical knowledge of healing to the sick and injured. There were no formal educational programs, and nursing "know how" was passed on informally from generation to generation.

The first U.S. school of nursing was established in 1872 at the New England Hospital for Women and Children in Boston. By 1898 there were schools of nursing in New York City and New Haven, Connecticut. In 1938, New York State passed the first state law to require that practical nurses be licensed.

World War II greatly affected the nursing field. More nurses were recruited during this war than at any other time in history. Thousands signed up for the Cadet Nurse Corps. Licensed practical nurses played a vital role in the treatment and care of thousands of soldiers.

In the 1940s, the National Association for Practical Nurse Education and Service (1941) and the National Federation of Licensed Practical Nurses (1949) were founded to promote quality patient care and represent the interests of licensed practical and licensed vocational nurses.

THE JOB

Licensed practical nurses work under the supervision of a registered nurse, or a physician. They are responsible for many general duties of nursing such as administering prescribed drugs and medical treatments to patients, taking patients' vital signs (temperature, blood pressure, pulse, respiration), dressing wounds, assisting in the preparation of medical examination and surgery, giving injections and enemas, and performing routine laboratory tests. LPNs help with therapeutic and rehabilitation sessions; they may also participate in the planning, practice, and evaluation of a patient's nursing care.

A primary duty of an LPN is to ensure that patients are clean and comfortable, and that their needs, both physical and emotional, are met. They sometimes assist patients with daily hygiene such as bathing, brushing teeth, and dressing. Many times they provide emotional comfort by simply talking with the patient.

LPNs working in nursing homes have duties similar to those employed by hospitals. They provide bedside care, administer medications, develop care plans, and supervise nurse assistants.

Top Employers and Mean Earnings, 2009

Employer	# Employed	Mean Earnings
Nursing care facilities	212,990	$42,320
General medical and surgical hospitals	158,390	$39,980
Offices of physicians	89,040	$36,770
Home health care services	64,250	$42,300
Community care facilities for the elderly	39,140	$41,950
Employment services	36,540	$46,190

Source: U.S. Department of Labor

Those working in doctors' offices and clinics are sometimes required to perform clerical duties such as keeping records, maintaining files and paperwork, as well as answering phones and tending the appointment book. Home health LPNs, in addition to their nursing duties, may sometimes prepare and serve meals to their patients. They also teach family members how to provide basic care for their loved ones when medical professionals are unavailable.

REQUIREMENTS

High School

Some LPN programs do not require a high school diploma, but it is highly recommended, particularly if you want to be eligible for advancement opportunities. To prepare for a career as an LPN, you should study biology, chemistry, physics, and science while in high school. English and mathematics courses are also helpful.

Postsecondary Training

Those interested in a career as an LPN usually enroll in a practical nursing program after graduating from high school. There are about 1,200 state-approved programs in the United States that provide practical nursing training. According to the U.S. Department of Labor (DOL), 60 percent of all LPNs graduate from a technical or vocational school and 30 percent from a community or junior college. The remainder are enrolled in colleges, hospital programs, or high schools. Most programs last 12 months, with time spent for both classroom study and supervised clinical care. Courses include basic nursing concepts, anatomy, physiology, pharmacology, medical-surgical nursing, pediatrics, obstetrics, nutrition, and first aid. Clinical practice is most often in a hospital setting.

Certification or Licensing

The National Federation of Licensed Practical Nurses offers voluntary certification for LPNs who specialize in IV therapy and gerontology. The National Association for Practical Nurse Education and Service offers voluntary certification for LPNs who specialize in long-term care or pharmacology. Contact these organizations for more information.

All 50 states require graduates of a state-approved practical nursing program to take the National Council Licensure Examination, which has been developed by the National Council of State Boards of Nursing.

Other Requirements

Stamina, both physical and mental, is a must for this occupation. LPNs may be assigned to care for heavy or immobile patients or patients confused with dementia. Patience, and a caring, nurturing attitude, are valuable qualities to possess in order to be a successful LPN. As part of a health care team, they must be able to follow orders and work under close supervision. Other important traits include good observational skills, strong decision-making abilities, and the ability to communication well with others.

EXPLORING

High school students can explore an interest in this career by reading books or by checking out Web sites devoted to the nursing field. You should also take advantage of any information available in your school career center. An excellent way to learn more about this career firsthand is to speak with the school nurse or local public health nurse. Visits to the local hospital can give you a feel for the work environment. Volunteer work at a hospital, community health center, or even the local Red Cross chapter can provide valuable experience. Some high schools offer membership in Future Nurses organizations.

EMPLOYERS

Approximately 753,600 licensed practical nurses are employed in the United States. The DOL reports that 28 percent of LPNs work in nursing facilities, 25 percent work in hospitals, and 12 percent work in physicians' offices and clinics. Others are employed by home health care agencies, public health agencies, schools, residential care facilities, temp agencies, and government agencies.

STARTING OUT

After they fulfill licensing requirements, LPNs should check with human resource departments of hospitals, nursing homes, and clinics for openings. Employment agencies that specialize in health professions, and state employment agencies are other ways to find employment, as are school career services offices. Newspaper classified ads, nursing associations, and professional journals are great sources of job opportunities.

ADVANCEMENT

About 40 percent of LPNs use their license and experience as a step-ping-stone for other occupations in the health field, many of which offer more responsibility and higher salaries. Some LPNs, for example, with additional training, become medical technicians, surgical attendants, optometric assistants, or psychiatric technicians. Many LPNs return to school to become registered nurses. Hospitals often offer LPNs the opportunity for more training, seminars, workshops, and clinical sessions to sharpen their nursing skills. Some LPNs pursue credentialing in specialties such as gerontology, long-term care, IV therapy, and pharmacology.

EARNINGS

According to the DOL, LPNs earned median annual salaries of $39,820 annually in 2009. Ten percent earned less than $28,890, and 10 percent earned more than $55,090. Many LPNs are able to supplement their salaries with overtime pay and shift differentials.

Licensed practical nurses who are employed full time also usually receive fringe benefits, such as paid sick, holiday, and vacation time, medical coverage, 401(k) plans, and other perks depending on the employer.

WORK ENVIRONMENT

Most LPNs work 40-hour weeks, less if part time. As with other health professionals, they may be asked to work during nights, weekends, or holidays to provide 24-hour care for their patients. Nurses are usually given pay differentials for these shifts. About 18 percent of LPNs work part time.

LPNs employed in hospitals and nursing homes, as well as in clinics, enjoy clean, well-lighted, and generally comfortable work environments. The nature of their work calls for LPNs to be on their feet for most of the shift—providing patient care, dispensing medication, or assisting other health personnel.

OUTLOOK

Employment for LPNs is expected to grow much faster than the average for all occupations through 2018, according to the DOL. A growing elderly population requiring long-term health care is the primary factor for the demand of qualified LPNs. Traditionally, hospitals have provided the most job opportunities for LPNs. However, this source will only provide a moderate number of openings in the future. Inpatient population is not expected to increase significantly. Also, in many hospitals, certified nursing attendants are increasingly taking over many of the duties of LPNs.

Employment is expected to be strongest for LPNs who work with the elderly in nursing care facilities, home health care services, and community care facilities. Due to advanced medical technology, people are living longer, though many will require medical assistance. Private medical practices will also be excellent job sources because many medical procedures are now being performed on an outpatient basis in doctors' offices. There will be many jobs in rural areas, where there is a shortage of LPNs and other health care professionals.

FOR MORE INFORMATION

For career and certification information, contact the following organizations:

National Association for Practical Nurse Education and Service
1940 Duke Street, Suite 200
Alexandria, VA 22314-3452
Tel: 703-933-1003
http://www.napnes.org

National Federation of Licensed Practical Nurses
605 Poole Drive
Garner, NC 27529-5203
Tel: 919-779-0046
http://www.nflpn.org

For information on licensing, contact
National Council of State Boards of Nursing
111 East Wacker Drive, Suite 2900
Chicago, IL 60601-4277
Tel: 312-525-3600
E-mail: info@ncsbn.org
https://www.ncsbn.org

Discover Nursing, sponsored by Johnson & Johnson Services Inc., provides information on nursing careers, nursing schools, and scholarships.

Discover Nursing
http://www.discovernursing.com

Neonatal Nurses

QUICK FACTS

School Subjects
Biology
Chemistry

Personal Interests
Helping/teaching
Technical/scientific

Work Environment
Primarily indoors
Primarily one location

Minimum Education Level
Some postsecondary training

Salary Range
$43,970 to $67,750 to
$93,700+

Certification or Licensing
Recommended (certification)
Required by all states
(licensing)

Outlook
Much faster than the average

DOT
075

GOE
14.02.01

NOC
3152

O*NET-SOC
29-1111.00, 29-1111.03

OVERVIEW

Neonatal nurses provide direct patient care to newborns in hospitals for the first month after birth. The babies they care for may be normal, they may be born prematurely, or they may be suffering from an illness or birth defect. Some of the babies require highly technical care such as surgery or the use of ventilators, incubators, or intravenous feedings.

HISTORY

Neonatal care in some basic form has been around since the dawn of time. But the specialized field of neonatal nursing did not develop until the 1960s as advancements in medical care and technology allowed for the improved treatment of premature babies. According to the March of Dimes, one of every 12 babies born in the United States annually suffers from low birth weight. Low birth weight is a factor in 65 percent of infant deaths. Neonatal nurses play a very important role in providing care for these infants, those born with birth defects or illness, and healthy babies.

THE JOB

Neonatal nurses care for newborn babies in hospitals. Depending on the size of the hospital, their duties may vary. Some neonatal nurses may be in the delivery room and, as soon as the baby is born, they clean up the baby, visually assess it, and draw blood by pricking the newborn's heel. This blood sample is sent to the laboratory, where a number of screening tests are performed as required by the state. These assessments help the staff and doctor determine if the baby is normal or needs additional testing, a special diet, or intensive care. Sharon Stout, RN, who was a neonatal nurse for six years in Georgia, said she loved being in the delivery room and caring for the newborn because she enjoyed seeing the interaction with the baby and the new mother and family. "It was usually a very happy time."

"However," she says, "if a baby needed special care that we could not provide at our facility, we stabilized it until the neonatal transport team arrived from a larger hospital to transfer the baby to its special neonatal care unit."

Babies who are born without complications are usually placed in a Level I nursery or in the mother's room with her. However, because of today's short hospital stays for mother and child, many hospitals no longer have Level I, or healthy baby, nurseries. Neonatal or general staff nurses help the new mothers care for their newborns in their hospital rooms.

Level II is a special care nursery for babies who have been born prematurely or who may have an illness, disease, or birth defect. These babies are also cared for by a neonatal nurse, or a staff nurse with more advanced training in caring for newborns. These babies may need oxygen, intravenous therapies, special feedings, or because of underdevelopment, they may simply need more time to mature.

Specialized neonatal nurses or more advanced degree nurses care for babies placed in the Level III neonatal intensive care unit. This unit admits all babies who cannot be treated in either of the other two nurseries. These at-risk babies require high-tech care such as ventilators, incubators, or surgery. Level III units are generally found in larger hospitals or may be part of a children's hospital.

REQUIREMENTS

High School

In order to become a neonatal nurse, you must first train to be a registered nurse. (See the article "Registered Nurses.") To prepare for a career as a registered nurse, you should take high school mathematics and science courses, including biology, chemistry, and physics. Health courses will also be helpful. English and speech courses should not be neglected because you must be able to communicate well with patients.

Postsecondary Training

There is no special program for neonatal nursing in basic RN education; however, some nursing programs have an elective course in neonatal nursing. Entry-level requirements to become a neonatal nurse depend on the institution, its size, and the availability of nurses in that specialty and geographical region. Some institutions may require neonatal nurses to demonstrate their ability in administering

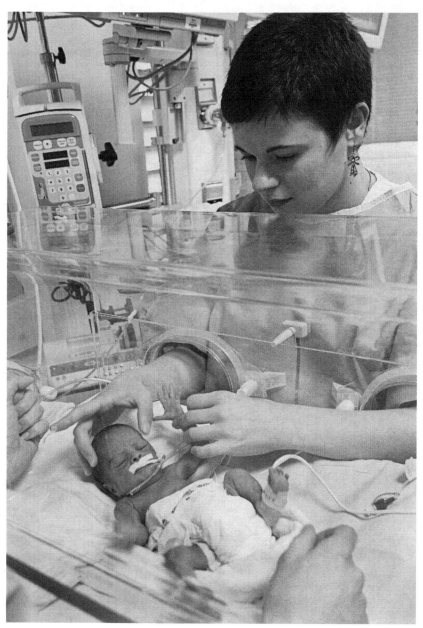

A neonatal nurse cares for a premature baby. *(Claude Paris, AP Photo)*

medications, performing necessary math calculations, suctioning, cardiopulmonary resuscitation, ventilator care, and other newborn care skills. Nurses who wish to focus on caring for premature babies or sick newborns may choose to attend graduate school to become a neonatal nurse practitioner or clinical nurse specialist.

Certification or Licensing

Neonatal nurses who work in critical care may become certified in neonatal critical care nursing by the AACN Certification Corporation, a subsidiary of the American Association of Critical Care Nurses (AACN). Applicants must have a minimum of 1,750 hours within the two years preceding application (with 875 hours in the year previous to application), pay an application fee, and take and pass an exam.

All states and the District of Columbia require a license to practice nursing. To obtain a license, graduates of approved nursing schools must pass a national examination. Nurses may be licensed by more than one state. In some states, continuing education is a condition for license renewal. Different titles require different education and training levels.

Other Requirements

Neonatal nurses should like working with mothers, newborns, and families. This is a very intense nursing field, especially when caring for the high-risk infant, so the neonatal nurse should be compassionate, patient, and able to handle stress and make decisions. The nurse should also be able to communicate well with other medical staff and the patients' families. Families of an at-risk newborn are often frightened and very worried about their infant. Because of their fears, family members may be difficult to deal with, and the nurse must display patience, understanding, and composure during these emotional times. The nurse must be able to communicate with the family and explain medical terminology and procedures to them so they understand what is being done for their baby and why.

EXPLORING

You can explore your interest in neonatal nursing by reading books on careers in nursing; by talking with high school counselors and neonatal nurses; and by visiting hospitals to observe a health care setting and talk with hospital personnel. Additionally, the Internet is full of resources about nursing. Check out Discover Nursing

(http://www.discovernursing.com), Nursing Net (http://www
.nursingnet.org), and the American Nurses Association's Nursing
World (http://www.nursingworld.org).

EMPLOYERS

Neonatal nurses are employed by hospitals, managed care facilities,
long-term care facilities, and government agencies.

STARTING OUT

The only way to become a registered nurse is through completion
of one of the three kinds of educational programs plus passing the
licensing examination. Registered nurses may apply for employment
directly to hospitals, nursing homes, and companies and government
agencies that hire nurses. Jobs can also be obtained through school
career services offices, by signing up with employment agencies specializing in placement of nursing personnel, or through the state
employment office. Other sources of jobs include nurses' associations (such as the National Association of Neonatal Nurses), professional journals, and newspaper want ads.

ADVANCEMENT

Neonatal nurses seeking career advancement, but who would like
to continue to care for babies, might consider becoming a neonatal nurse practitioner or clinical nurse specialist. They can do this
by gaining at least two years of experience in a neonatal intensive
care unit (recommended by the National Association of Neonatal Nurses) and then completing graduate school training in their
desired specialty.

EARNINGS

Salary is determined by many factors, including nursing specialty,
education, and place of employment, shift worked, geographic location, and work experience. According to the U.S. Department of
Labor (DOL), registered nurses working at hospitals had a median
annual income of $67,750 in 2009. The lowest paid 10 percent of
all registered nurses earned less than $43,970 per year. The high-
est paid 10 percent made more than $93,700. However, neonatal
specialty nurses can generally expect to earn more, especially when

advancing to administrative positions. According to the National Association of Neonatal Nurses, nurses just starting out in this field may have starting salaries in the upper $30,000s to mid-$40,000s. Given these high beginning salaries, it is logical to expect a neonatal nurse with some experience to earn more than the national median for all registered nurses.

Flexible schedules and part-time employment opportunities are available for most nurses. Employers usually provide health and life insurance, and some offer educational reimbursements and year-end bonuses to their full-time staff.

WORK ENVIRONMENT

Neonatal nurses can expect to work in a hospital environment that is clean and well lighted. Inner-city hospitals may be in a less than desirable location, and safety may be an issue. Generally, neonatal nurses who wish to advance in their careers will find themselves working in larger hospitals in major cities.

Nurses usually spend much of the day on their feet, either walking or standing. Many hospital nurses work 10- or 12-hour shifts, which can be tiring. Long hours and intense nursing demands can create burnout for some nurses, meaning that they often become dissatisfied with their jobs. Fortunately, there are many areas in which nurses can use their skills, so sometimes trying a different type of nursing may be the answer.

OUTLOOK

The DOL predicts that employment for all registered nurses will grow much faster than the average for all careers through 2018. In addition, nursing specialties should be in great demand in the future. The outlook for neonatal nurses is excellent, especially for those with master's degrees or higher.

FOR MORE INFORMATION

For information on educational programs, contact
American Association of Colleges of Nursing
One Dupont Circle, NW, Suite 530
Washington, DC 20036-1135
Tel: 202-463-6930
http://www.aacn.nche.edu

For information on certification and fact sheets on critical care nursing, contact

American Association of Critical-Care Nurses
101 Columbia
Aliso Viejo, CA 92656-4109
Tel: 800-899-2226
E-mail: info@aacn.org
http://www.aacn.org

For information on neonatal nursing, contact

Association of Women's Health, Obstetric and Neonatal Nurses
2000 L Street, NW, Suite 740
Washington, DC 20036-4912
Tel: 800-673-8499
http://www.awhonn.org

For career information and job listings, contact

National Association of Neonatal Nurses
4700 West Lake Avenue
Glenview, IL 60025-1468
Tel: 800-451-3795
E-mail: info@nann.org
http://www.nann.org

Nurse Anesthetists

OVERVIEW

Nurse anesthetists, also known as *certified registered nurse anesthetists (CRNAs)*, are one of four classifications of advanced practice nurses (APNs). They are registered nurses (RNs) with advanced training in anesthesiology. They are responsible for administering, supervising, and monitoring anesthesia-related care for patients undergoing surgical procedures. General anesthesia is not necessary for all surgical procedures; therefore, nurse anesthetists also work on cases in which they provide various types of local anesthesia—topical, infiltration, nerve-block, spinal, and epidural or caudal. There are approximately 49,000 nurse anesthetists working in the United States.

HISTORY

Reliable methods of putting a patient to sleep were first developed in the 1840s, when the discovery of ether anesthesia revolutionized surgery. Before that time, when surgery offered the only possible chance of saving a person's life, all that the surgeon could do was give alcohol or opium to deaden the pain. Similarly, mandrake, hemp, and herbane may have been given orally, or by inhalation, during childbirth.

The first nurse anesthetist was Sister Mary Bernard, who practiced in Pennsylvania in the 1870s. The first school of nurse anesthetists was founded in 1909 at St. Vincent Hospital in Portland, Oregon. Since then, many schools have been established, and the nurse anesthesia specialty was formally created on June 17, 1931, when the American Association of Nurse Anesthetists held its first meeting.

QUICK FACTS

School Subjects
Biology
Chemistry

Personal Skills
Helping/teaching
Technical/scientific

Work Environment
Primarily indoors
Primarily multiple locations

Minimum Education Level
Master's degree

Salary Range
$135,752 to $154,567 to
$198,435+

Certification or Licensing
Required

Outlook
Much faster than the average

DOT
075

GOE
14.02.01

NOC
3152

O*NET-SOC
29-1111.02

Contemporary anesthesiology is far more complicated and much more effective than in the early days when an ether- or chloroform-soaked cloth or sponge was held up to the patient's face. Today, a combination of several modern-day anesthetic agents is usually used to anesthetize the patient.

THE JOB

According to the American Association of Nurse Anesthetists, certified nurse anesthetists administer approximately 30 million anesthetic procedures annually. In more than two-thirds of rural hospitals, nurse anesthetists are the only anesthesia providers.

Nurse anesthetists are clearly important members of health care teams across the country. Prior to surgery, a nurse anesthetist takes the patient's history, evaluates his or her anesthesia needs, and forms a plan for the best possible management of the case (often in consultation with an anesthesiologist). The nurse anesthetist also explains the planned procedures to the patient and answers questions the patient might have. Prior to the operation, the nurse anesthetist administers an intravenous (IV) sedative to relax the patient. Then the nurse anesthetist administers a combination of drugs to establish and maintain the patient in a controlled state of unconsciousness, insensibility to pain, and muscular relaxation. Some general anesthetics are administered by inhalation through a mask and tube, and others are administered intravenously. Because the muscular relaxants prevent patients from breathing on their own, the nurse anesthetist has to provide artificial respiration through a tube inserted into the windpipe. Throughout the surgery, the nurse anesthetist monitors the patient's vital signs by watching the video and digital displays. The nurse anesthetist is also responsible for maintaining the patient's blood, water, and salt levels as well as continually readjusting the flow of anesthetics and other medications to ensure optimal results. After surgery, nurse anesthetists monitor the patient's return to consciousness and watch for complications. The nurse anesthetists must be skilled in the use of airways, ventilators, IVs, blood- and fluid-replacement techniques, and postoperative pain management.

REQUIREMENTS

High School

If you want to become a nurse anesthetist, you will first need to become a registered nurse. To prepare for this career, you should take high school mathematics and science courses, including biology,

Facts About Certified Nurse Anesthetists

- Certified nurse anesthetists are the sole anesthesia providers in more than two–thirds of all rural hospitals in the United States. Their work allows 70 million rural Americans to have access to health care procedures that require anesthesia.
- Approximately 41 percent of certified nurse anesthetists are men, compared to only 10 percent of the entire nursing profession.
- Today, anesthesia care is almost 50 times safer than it was two decades ago.

Source: American Association of Nurse Anesthetists

chemistry, and physics. Health courses will also be helpful. English and speech courses should not be neglected because you must be able to communicate well with patients.

Postsecondary Training

All applicants to nurse anesthetist programs must be registered nurses with a bachelor's degree and have at least one year's acute care nursing experience. More than 100 programs have been recognized by the Council of Accreditation of Nurse Anesthesia Educational Programs. The American Association of Nurse Anesthetists (AANA) provides a listing of these programs at its Web site, http://www.aana.com. Admission is competitive, and programs last 24 to 36 months. All accredited programs offer at least a master's degree, and some offer a post-master's certificate or a doctorate. Students take extensive classes in pharmacology and the sciences. They also participate in anesthesia-related clinical experience in surgery and obstetrics. According to the AANA, the average student nurse anesthetist "works at least 1,694 clinical hours and administers more than 790 anesthetics."

Certification or Licensing

All registered nurses must be licensed to practice in the United States. In addition, nurse anesthetists are required to pass a national certification exam given by the Council on Certification of Nurse Anesthetists. All states recognize certified registered nurse anesthetist (CRNA) status. Certified nurse anesthetists are not required to work under the supervision of an anesthesiologist, although some licensing laws do stipulate that they must work with a physician.

CRNAs must be recertified every two years according to the criteria established by the Council on Recertification of Nurse Anesthetists. Part of this requirement includes earning 40 continuing education credits every two years. The American Society of Peri-Anesthesia Nurses also offers a certification program.

Other Requirements

Nurse anesthetists must have the ability to concentrate for long periods of time and remain focused on monitoring their patient during surgery. They must be able to analyze problems accurately and swiftly, make decisions quickly, and react appropriately. They must have the ability to remain calm during emergencies and be able to handle stressful situations.

Nurse anesthetists also need to have efficient time management skills in order to work efficiently with surgeons and their operating schedules.

EXPLORING

Books, nursing association Web sites, and information interviews with nurses will provide you with more information about nursing careers. You can also learn more about nurse anesthetists by visiting the About the Profession section of the AANA Web site (http://www .aana.com/abouttheprofession.aspx).

EMPLOYERS

The *Occupational Outlook Handbook* reports there are 49,000 nurse anesthetists working in the United States. Many nurse anesthetists are employed by hospitals or outpatient surgery centers. Dentists, podiatrists, ophthalmologists, plastic surgeons, and pain management specialists also employ them. Others may be employed in a group or independent practice that provides services to hospitals and other health care centers on a contract basis. Some work for rural hospitals, the U.S. Public Health Service Commissioned Corps, the Department of Veterans Affairs, and the U.S. military. Because the high-quality, cost-effective anesthesia service provided by nurse anesthetists is widely acknowledged, health care institutions are eager to employ them.

STARTING OUT

Nurse anesthetists may apply for employment directly to hospitals, outpatient surgery centers, and government agencies that hire nurses. Jobs can also be obtained through school career services offices, by signing up with employment agencies specializing in placement of nursing personnel, or through the state employment office. Other sources of jobs include nurses' associations, employment and social networking Web sites, professional journals, and newspaper want ads.

ADVANCEMENT

Nurse anesthetists who want new professional challenges beyond direct practice might consider teaching or administrative positions or involvement in research for improved or specialized anesthesia equipment and procedures. Some nurse anesthetists choose to acquire other advanced-practice nursing qualifications so they can be involved in a wider range of nursing activities. Doctoral programs for nurse anesthetists are expected to expand in the near future.

EARNINGS

Nurse anesthetists are among the highest paid nursing specialists. Earnings vary based on type and size of employer, years of experience, and location, among other factors. Salary.com reports that in November 2010, the average salary for nurse anesthetists was $154,567, with salaries ranging from a low of $135,752 to more than $175,105. Chief nurse anesthetists earned salaries that ranged from less than $146,574 to $198,435 or more.

Fringe benefits are usually similar to other full-time health care workers and may include sick leave, vacation, health and life insurance, and tuition assistance.

WORK ENVIRONMENT

Nurse anesthetists usually work in sterile, well-lighted operating facilities. They spend considerable time on their feet and may be required to stand for many hours at a time. Emergencies can produce a stressful and fast-paced environment. Many nurse anesthetists must be on call, usually on a rotation basis, to respond to emergency surgical situations.

OUTLOOK

The American Association of Nurse Anesthetists predicts a bright future for CRNAs. In addition, the U.S. Department of Labor projects employment for all registered nurses to grow much faster than the average for all careers through 2018. Strong demand for CRNAs will result from several factors. For example, there is currently a shortage of CRNAs in the marketplace. Also, with the continuing trend of cutting costs in all health care facilities, CRNAs will be in demand to provide an alternative to hiring higher-priced anesthesiologists. The increased use of managed health care services and the aging population will also result in a need for additional nurse anesthetists.

FOR MORE INFORMATION

For comprehensive information on the career of nurse anesthetist, contact

American Association of Nurse Anesthetists
222 South Prospect Avenue
Park Ridge, IL 60068-4001
Tel: 847-692-7050
E-mail: info@aana.com
http://www.aana.com

For information on certification, contact

American Society of PeriAnesthesia Nurses
90 Frontage Road
Cherry Hill, NJ 08034-1424
Tel: 877-737-9696
E-mail: aspan@aspan.org
http://www.aspan.org

For general information, contact

National League for Nursing
61 Broadway, 33rd Floor
New York, NY 10006-2701
Tel: 212-363-5555
E-mail: generalinfo@nln.org
http://www.nln.org

Discover Nursing, sponsored by Johnson & Johnson Services Inc., provides information on nursing careers, nursing schools, and scholarships.

Discover Nursing
http://www.discovernursing.com

================= **INTERVIEW** =================

James Walker, CRNA, DNP, is the director of the Graduate Program in Nurse Anesthesia and an associate professor of anesthesiology and allied health sciences at Baylor College of Medicine in Houston, Texas. He works in clinical practice at Ben Taub General Hospital, a Level 1 Trauma Center. He is also the president of the American Association of Nurse Anesthetists. James discussed his career and the field of nurse anesthesia with the editors of Careers in Focus: Nursing.

Q. How long have you worked in the field?

A. I became a registered nurse in 1982, and obtained a master of science degree in nurse anesthesia in 1992. I have been practicing as a certified registered nurse anesthetist (CRNA) since that time.

Q. What made you want to enter this career?

A. The profession of nurse anesthesia is very challenging and rewarding. Providing anesthesia care is a logical progression from the type of care provided in the intensive care unit. There are a variety of technical skills that were attractive such as endotracheal intubation, central venous line insertion, spinal anesthesia, and epidural catheter insertion. The autonomy afforded to nurse anesthetists was very attractive, in that we are allowed to utilize our knowledge and skills to the extent of our education. Anesthesia care involves making split-second decisions, and requires the integration of patient assessment data as well as clinical knowledge and judgment. The most rewarding aspect of anesthesia practice for me is knowing that I have the knowledge, skill, and abilities to provide safe and effective care to patients undergoing surgical and obstetric procedures.

Q. What is one thing that young people may not know about a career as a nurse anesthetist?

A. Nurse anesthesia is one of the most exciting and demanding advanced practice registered nursing specialties. Approximately 80 percent of nurse anesthetists practice with anesthesiologists, while the remainder practices independently. Nurse anesthetists are the sole anesthesia providers in the vast majority of rural hospitals. If not for nurse anesthetists, most rural hospitals would not be able to offer surgical, obstetric, and trauma stabilization services. There are 110 nurse anesthesia educational programs in the United States. Nurse anesthesia education is at the graduate level, offering either a master's or doctoral degree upon completion of the program. Nurse anesthetists must pass the National Certification Examination offered by the National Board on Certification and Recertification of Nurse Anesthetists to become a CRNA Recertification is required every two years. The majority of states require CRNAs to hold a current RN license and also be recognized (e.g., licensed, authorized) as advanced practice registered nurses. CRNAs are among the highest paid nurses in the United States, which is commensurate with their level of education and patient care responsibilities.

Q. What are the most important personal and professional qualities for nurse anesthetists?

A. CRNAs typically are intelligent, highly motivated, achievement-oriented, assertive, and autonomous individuals. They enjoy working hard, and are comfortable with a high level of responsibility for patient care. The American Association of Nurse Anesthetists (AANA) has identified the profession's values as integrity, professionalism, advocacy, and quality. Nurse anesthetists must possess a strong sense of integrity, and continuously demonstrate professionalism. They are strong advocates not only for their patients, but also for their profession. Achieving the highest quality of care is paramount to CRNAs.

Q. What are some of the pros and cons of your job?

A. Being a CRNA affords nurses a very high level of responsibility and autonomy. That level of responsibility results in a high degree of professional satisfaction and reward. Patients, families, and surgeons are grateful for the CRNA's talents and skills. In addition, compensation for CRNA services provides a comfortable lifestyle.

CRNAs must be committed to provide anesthesia services 24/7/365. Anesthesia care is needed, many times on an emergency basis, at all hours of the day and night. This requires CRNAs to be available on nights and weekends, and many times work very long hours. This can interfere with family and social agendas at times. Because CRNAs possess such special skills and abilities, this level of commitment is simply part of the professional culture.

Q. **What advice would you give to young people who are interested in the field?**

A. Nurse anesthesia is a wonderful profession, extremely rewarding, and affords a nice lifestyle. Becoming a nurse anesthetist is not easy, and requires demonstrated academic and clinical excellence. Aspiring nurse anesthetists must possess very competitive undergraduate grades, and have excellent clinical experience to effectively compete for the limited positions available in nurse anesthesia educational programs. Most programs have three to four applicants for each position in the program. Only the most competitive applicants will be successful.

Q. **What is the future outlook for nurse anesthetists?**

A. The future for nurse anesthetists is very bright. The long history of excellence in nurse anesthesia care for nearly 150 years will lead to increased utilization of nurse anesthetists. CRNAs have demonstrated that they are the most cost-effective of all anesthesia providers. The quality of nurse anesthesia care is well documented, demonstrating a high level of safety regardless of whether the CRNA practices independently or with an anesthesiologist. As the United States embraces health reform, it is clear that CRNAs are an integral and cost-effective solution for our health care system.

Nurse Assistants

QUICK FACTS

School Subjects
Biology
Health

Personal Skills
Following instructions
Helping/teaching

Work Environment
Primarily indoors
Primarily multiple locations

Minimum Education Level
High school diploma

Salary Range
$17,510 to $24,040 to
$33,970+

Certification or Licensing
Required for certain
positions

Outlook
Faster than the average

DOT
354

GOE
14.07.01

NOC
3413

O*NET-SOC
31-1012.00

OVERVIEW

Nurse assistants (also called *nurse aides, orderlies,* or *hospital attendants*) work under the supervision of nurses and handle much of the personal care needs of the patients. This allows the nursing staff to perform their primary duties more effectively and efficiently. Nurse assistants help move patients, assist in patients' exercise and nutrition needs, and oversee patients' personal hygiene. Nurse assistants may also be required to take patients to other areas of the hospital for treatment, therapy, or diagnostic testing. They are required to keep charts of their work with their patients for review by other medical personnel and to comply with required reporting. There are about 1.5 million nurse assistants in the United States, and about 41 percent of them are employed in nursing care facilities.

HISTORY

From earliest times, healthy people have been called upon to care for the sick and injured. Methods for dealing with illness exist in all societies and are a necessity for any type of community life. The social and economic development of societies throughout history has been closely tied to the fundamental need to tend to the needs of the unwell.

To care for the sick in their midst, early Greek, Indian, Chinese, Aztec, and other civilizations established special caregiving places resembling today's hospices and hospitals. The spread of Christianity gave new impetus to efforts for caring for the sick. Monasteries had infirmaries for their own sick members, and they welcomed pilgrims and travelers who were ill to use their facilities. Military and chivalric groups also tended to the sick with hospital and charity work. Two hospitals were founded in the 11th century in Jerusalem by the Knights Hospitallers of St. John, who cared for both the mentally ill and the physically ill.

As the practice of medicine has become more complex, the need for nurses—and consequently nursing aides—grew. In the 19th century a nurse named Florence Nightingale led a movement for reform in nursing. In 1873 the first school of nursing in the United States was established in New York City at Bellevue Hospital.

The increased burden on trained nurses has made nursing aides irreplaceable. Aides provide basic care for those who are incapacitated or who need the same services regularly, which frees nurses and doctors to minister to their patients' diseases.

THE JOB

Nurse assistants generally help nurses care for patients in hospital or nursing home settings. Their duties include tending to the daily care of the patients, including bathing them, helping them with their meals, and checking their body temperature and blood pressure. In addition, they often help persons who need assistance with their personal hygiene needs and answer their call lights when they need immediate assistance.

The work can be strenuous, requiring the lifting and moving of patients. Nurse assistants must work with partners or in groups when performing the more strenuous tasks to ensure their safety as well as the patient's. Some requirements of the job can be as routine

Facts About Nurse Assistants

- Career nurse assistants provide 80 to 90 percent of the care in long-term care facilities.
- Approximately 276,000 new jobs are expected to be available for nurse assistants from 2008 to 2018.
- In 2009, top-paying states for nurse assistants were: Alaska ($32,390), Nevada ($30,970), New York ($30,850), Hawaii ($30,500), and Connecticut ($30,040).

Source: Career Nurse Assistants Programs, U.S. Department of Labor

as changing sheets and helping a patient or resident with phone calls, while other requirements can be as difficult and unpleasant as assisting a resident with elimination and cleaning up a resident or patient who has vomited.

Nurse assistants may be called upon to perform the more menial and unappealing tasks of health and personal care, but they also have the opportunity to develop meaningful relationships with patients. In a nursing home, nursing assistants work closely with residents, often gaining their trust and friendship.

REQUIREMENTS

High School
Although a high school diploma is not always required to work as a nurse assistant, there are a number of high school classes that can help you do this work. Communication skills are valuable for a nurse assistant to have, so take English classes. Science courses, such as biology and anatomy, and family and consumer science, health, and nutrition classes are also helpful. Some high schools offer courses directly related to nurse assistant training. These classes may include body mechanics, infection control, and resident/patient rights.

Postsecondary Training
Nurse assistants are not required to have a college degree, but they may have to complete a short training course at a community college or vocational school. These training courses, usually taught by a registered nurse, teach basic nursing skills and prepare students for the state certification exam. Nurse assistants typically begin the training courses after getting their first job as an assistant, and the course work is often incorporated into their on-the-job training.

Many people work as nurse assistants as they pursue other medical professions such as a premedical or nursing program.

Certification or Licensing
Some states require nurse assistants to be certified no matter where they work. The Omnibus Budget Reconciliation Act of 1987 requires nurse assistants working in nursing homes to undergo special training. Nursing homes can hire inexperienced workers as nurse assistants, but they must have at least 75 hours of training and pass a competency evaluation program within four months of being hired. Those who fulfill these requirements are known as certified nurse assistants.

A nurse assistant holds a glass of water for an elderly woman, who is taking her daily medication. *(Sonda Dawes, The Image Works)*

Other Requirements

You must care about the patients in your care, and you must show a genuine understanding and compassion for the ill, the disabled, and the elderly. Because of the rigorous physical demands placed on you, you should be in good health and have good work habits. Along with good physical health, you should have good mental health and a cheerful disposition. The job can be emotionally demanding, requiring patience and stability. You should be able to work as a part of a team and also be able to take orders and follow through on your responsibilities.

EXPLORING

Because a high school diploma is frequently not required of nursing aides, many high school students are hired by nursing homes and hospitals for part-time work. Job opportunities may also exist in a hospital or nursing home kitchen, introducing you to diet and nutrition. These jobs will give you an opportunity to become familiar with the hospital and nursing home environments. Also, volunteer work can familiarize you with the work nurses and nurse assistants perform, as well as introduce you to basic medical terminology.

EMPLOYERS

Approximately 41 percent of the 1.5 million nurse assistants in the United States are employed in nursing homes. Twenty-nine percent work in hospitals. Others work in halfway houses, retirement centers, homes for persons with disabilities, and private homes.

STARTING OUT

Because of the high demand for nurse assistants, you can apply directly to the health facilities in your area, contact your local employment office, or check your local newspaper's help wanted ads.

ADVANCEMENT

For the most part, there is not much opportunity for advancement within the position of nurse assistant. To advance in a health care facility requires additional training. After becoming familiar with the medical and nursing home environments and gaining some knowledge of medical terminology, some nurse assistants enroll in nursing programs or pursue other medically related careers.

Many facilities are recognizing the need to retain good health care workers and are putting some training and advancement programs in place for their employees.

EARNINGS

Salaries for most health care professionals vary by region, population, and size and kind of institution. The pay for nurse assistants in a hospital is usually more than in a nursing home.

According to the U.S. Department of Labor (DOL), nurse assistants earned median hourly wages of $11.56 in 2009. For full-time work at 40 hours per week, this hourly wage translates into a yearly income of approximately $24,040. The lowest paid 10 percent earned less than $8.42 per hour (approximately $17,510 per year), and the highest paid 10 percent earned more than $16.33 per hour (approximately $33,970 annually).

Benefits are usually based on the hours worked, length of employment, and the policies of the facility. Some offer paid vacation and holidays, medical or hospital insurance, and retirement plans. Some also provide free meals to their workers.

WORK ENVIRONMENT

The work environment in a health care or long-term care facility can be hectic at times and very stressful. Some patients may be uncooperative and may actually be combative. Often there are numerous demands that must be met at the same time. Nurse assistants are required to be on their feet most of the time, and they often have to help lift or move patients. Most facilities are clean and well lighted, but nurse assistants do have the possibility of exposure to contagious diseases, although using proper safety procedures minimizes their risk.

Nurse assistants generally work a 40-hour workweek, with some overtime. The hours and weekly schedule may be irregular, depending on the needs of the institution. Nurse assistants are needed around the clock, so work schedules may include night shift or swing-shift work.

OUTLOOK

The DOL predicts that employment for nurse assistants will grow faster than the average for all careers through 2018. Because of the physical and emotional demands of the job, and because of the lack of advancement opportunities, there is a high employee turnover rate in this field. Additional opportunities may be available as different types of care facilities are developed and as facilities try to curb operating costs. Opportunities will be best in nursing and long-term care facilities.

In addition, more nurse assistants will be required as government and private agencies develop more programs to assist the disabled, dependent people, and the increasing elderly population.

FOR MORE INFORMATION

For information and statistics on the home health care industry, visit the association's Web site.

National Association for Home Care and Hospice
228 Seventh Street, SE
Washington, DC 20003-4306
Tel: 202-547-7424
http://www.nahc.org

For information on careers at nursing homes, contact

National Association of Health Care Assistants
2709 West 13th Street
Joplin, MO 64801-3663
Tel: 800-784-6049
E-mail: info@nahcacares.org
http://www.nahcacares.org

For additional information on nurse assistant careers and training, contact

National Network of Career Nursing Assistants
Tel: 330-825-9342
E-mail: cnajeni@aol.com
http://www.cna-network.org

Nurse Managers

OVERVIEW

Nurse managers are experienced health care professionals who manage the operations of services and personnel in medical offices, hospitals, nursing homes, community health programs, institutions, and other places where health care is provided. Their responsibilities vary depending on their position and place of employment. They may be in charge of hiring and firing their staff, as well as evaluating their performance. They are usually responsible for maintaining patient and departmental records, including government and insurance documents. They may develop and maintain budgets. Nurse managers are often in charge of establishing, implementing, and enforcing departmental policies.

Some nurse managers provide nursing care to patients along with managing the floor or unit. They are referred to as *charge nurses* or *working managers*.

HISTORY

Before the 19th century, the care of sick and injured individuals was provided by concerned individuals who nursed rather than by trained nurses. They had not received the kind of training that is required for nurses today.

The first school of nursing in the United States was founded in Boston in 1873. In 1938, New York State passed the first state law to require that practical nurses be licensed. After the law was passed, a movement began to have organized training programs that would assure new standards in the field. The role and training of nurses have undergone radical changes since the first schools were opened. Education standards for nurses have been improving constantly since that time. Today's nurse is a highly educated, licensed health care professional.

Nurse managers have always been needed to manage nurses and nursing departments. They serve as an important link between health care management and nurses. In 1967, the American Organization of Nurse Executives, a subsidiary of the American Hospital Association, was formed as an advocacy group for nurses who "design, facilitate, and manage care." Today, it has a membership of more than 7,000 nurses.

THE JOB

Nurse managers are leaders in the health field. They are the professionals responsible for managing the staff that cares for patients. They are also in charge of the operation of their department or unit, and they perform administrative duties related to patient care.

Debbie Robertson-Huffman has more than 20 years of operating room experience and is currently director of surgical services for a 100-bed hospital in California. She is in charge of five departments within the surgical unit: central processing, operating room staff, ambulatory surgery, recovery room, and special procedures, such as endoscopies.

Being in charge means she is responsible for all of the staffing and scheduling of her employees, scheduling the operating and special procedures rooms, and ultimately for the smooth operation of the entire surgical unit.

Although it is demanding, Robertson-Huffman enjoys her job. She loves working with her staff. "I have the greatest people working for me," she brags. "The dependable staff I have in all my departments makes it an easy job for me. Our group is like one big, happy family—with its dysfunctional moments," she laughs.

"Nurse managers need to be people persons," notes Robertson-Huffman. "They must believe in teamwork and that every member of the team is essential and that no one is more, or less, important than someone else."

Although working with people is a plus, the paperwork involved is a minus. "It is so cumbersome," says Robertson-Huffman. "Someone is always needing a report or statistics. We are losing sight of the people with all of the report requirements."

Nurse managers are responsible for many aspects of the smooth operation of their unit. "I liked having the ability to get things accomplished," says Sharon Stout, a nurse manager of a small pediatrics

Learn More About It

Finkler, Steven A., Christine T. Kovner, and Cheryl B. Jones. *Financial Management for Nurse Managers and Executives*. 3d ed. St. Louis, Mo.: Saunders, 2007.

Marrelli, T. M. *Nurse Manager's Survival Guide: Practical Answers to Everyday Problems*. 3d ed. St. Louis: Mosby, 2004.

McEachen, Irene. *Nurse Management Demystified*. New York: McGraw-Hill Professional, 2006.

Swansburg, Russell C., and Richard J. Swansburg. *Introduction to Management and Leadership for Nurse Managers*. 3d ed. Sudbury, Mass.: Jones & Bartlett Publishers, 2002.

unit for four years. "I saw what needed to be done and knew who to call and what to do to get it done. I liked that."

Some nurse managers are working nurse managers, meaning that they also care directly for patients along with managing the department. Robertson-Huffman will often help out in the operating room, or as she calls it, "the heart of the OR," when she is needed. Stout was also a working nurse manager. She says the size of the facility usually determines if the nurse manager also cares for patients. "I liked being a working nurse manager," she says, "because it put me in contact with the patients and their families."

Nurse managers work long hours and are usually on call. Robertson-Huffman works eight- to 10-hour shifts, five days a week, and she is always on call for situations that might arise. "Nurse managers need to have stamina," she notes.

In addition, downsizing at some health care facilities and mergers of institutions may mean additional responsibilities for nurse managers.

REQUIREMENTS

High School

If you want to become a nurse manager you will first need to become a registered nurse. (See the article "Registered Nurses.") To prepare for this career, you should take high school mathematics and science courses, including biology, chemistry, and physics. Health courses will also be helpful. English and speech courses should not be neglected because you must be able to communicate well with patients.

Postsecondary Training

All nurse managers begin their careers as registered nurses. The two most common ways to become a registered nurse are to get a bachelor's degree in nursing from an accredited four-year program or to get an associate's degree in nursing from an accredited two-year program. Additionally, some people train for nursing careers via diploma programs. Bachelor's or advanced degrees may be required for some nurse manager positions. Nurse managers need to have considerable clinical nursing experience and previous management experience.

Some nurses combine their nursing degree with a business degree, or they take business studies or health care management courses to advance to higher management positions such as directors, health care executives, or administrators.

Certification or Licensing

The American Organization of Nurse Executives offers the following certifications to nurse managers: certified in executive nursing practice and certified nurse manager and leader (which was developed in partnership with the American Association of Critical Care Nurses). Contact the organization for information on certification requirements.

All states and the District of Columbia require nurses to have a license to practice nursing. To obtain a license, graduates of approved nursing schools must pass a national examination. Nurses may be licensed by more than one state. In some states, continuing education is a condition for license renewal. Different titles require different education and training levels.

Other Requirements

Nurse managers must be good people managers and have the ability to work with all levels of employees and management, as well as patients and their families. They should have excellent organizational and leadership skills, and be able to make intelligent decisions in a fast-paced environment. They must also be assertive and demand that procedures are done correctly and quickly. They often need to set policies and see that they are followed and documented. New medical technologies and patient treatments are constantly being developed and implemented, so nurse managers must stay abreast of new information in the medical field. They also need to stay up-to-date on new insurance and government regulations and reporting requirements.

EXPLORING

There are many ways to learn more about nursing. You can go to your school or local library and check out books on nursing, or you can visit the Web sites of nursing associations (see the end of this article for contact information). You might also ask your teacher or school counselor to set up a presentation by a nurse or nurse manager.

You might also consider volunteering at a hospital or other health care facility. This will allow you to see nurses on the job. Some schools offer participation in Future Nurses programs. If you are interested in becoming a nurse manager, you might consider managing a school club, organization, or intramural sports team. This experience will teach you how to manage people, keep records, and maintain budgets.

EMPLOYERS

Nurse managers are employed by medical offices, hospitals, nursing homes, community health programs, managed care facilities, long-term care facilities, clinics, industry, private homes, schools, camps, and government agencies.

STARTING OUT

The position of nurse manager is not an entry-level position. Only experienced, well-trained nurses are trusted to manage other nurses as well as the health of patients. To begin your career path to nurse manager, you will first need to become a registered nurse. Registered nurses may apply for employment directly to hospitals, nursing homes and companies and government agencies that hire nurses. Jobs can also be obtained through school career services offices, by signing up with employment agencies specializing in placement of nursing personnel, or through the state employment office. Other sources of jobs include professional journals and newspaper want ads. Additionally, the American Organization of Nurse Executives offers job listings at its Web site, http://www.aone.org/aone/edandcareer/career_center.html.

ADVANCEMENT

Nurse managers may advance by taking positions at larger facilities with higher budgets and more staff. They may also pursue advanced degrees in health care administration, which would allow them to manage nursing homes, hospitals, and other health care facilities.

EARNINGS

Educational background, experience, responsibilities, and geographic location determine earnings as a nurse manager.

According to the U.S. Department of Labor (DOL), the median annual earnings of all registered nurses were $63,750 in 2009. Salaries ranged from less than $43,970 to more than $93,700 a year. Nurse managers, however, can usually expect to make more. The DOL reports that medical and health service managers who supervised nursing care facilities earned mean annual salaries of $77,560 in 2009. Head nurses earned salaries that ranged from less than $63,147 to $95,142 or more in November 2010, according to Salary.com.

Employers usually provide health and life insurance, paid vacation and sick leave and retirement plans, and some offer reimbursements for continuing education expenses.

WORK ENVIRONMENT

Nurse managers can work in any number of health care facilities, including doctor's offices, medical clinics, hospitals, institutions, and nursing homes, as well as other medical facilities. Most health care environments are clean and well lighted. Inner-city facilities in economically distressed areas may be in less than desirable locations, and safety may be an issue.

All health-related careers have some health and disease risks; however, adherence to health and safety guidelines greatly minimizes the chance of contracting infectious diseases such as hepatitis and AIDS. Medical knowledge and good safety measures are also needed to limit exposure to toxic chemicals, radiation, and other hazards.

OUTLOOK

Nursing specialties will be in great demand in the future. The DOL predicts that employment for all types of registered nurses will grow much faster than the average for all careers through 2018. As the number of nurses increases, more nurse managers will be needed to supervise these workers.

FOR MORE INFORMATION

For information on accredited educational programs, contact
American Association of Colleges of Nursing
One Dupont Circle, NW, Suite 530
Washington, DC 20036-1135
Tel: 202-463-6930
http://www.aacn.nche.edu

For information on careers, contact
American Organization of Nurse Executives
Liberty Place
325 Seventh Street, NW
Washington, DC 20004-2818
Tel: 202-626-2240
E-mail: aone@aha.org
http://www.aone.org

Nurse-Midwives

OVERVIEW

Certified nurse-midwives are registered nurses with advanced training who assist in family planning, pregnancy, and childbirth. They also provide routine health care for women. Nurse-midwives work in hospitals, with physicians in private practice, in freestanding birth centers or well-woman care centers, in women's clinics, and even in the homes of clients. There are more than 11,540 nurse-midwives in the United States. Certified nurse-midwives attend 7.4 percent of all U.S. births.

HISTORY

Before the relatively recent inventions of pain medication, hospitals, and medical intervention, for centuries women gave birth at home, guided by other women who were designated assistants, or midwives. Midwife means "with woman," and early midwives, like today's professional nurse-midwives, coached mothers-to-be through their pregnancy and labor. They helped women deliver their babies and taught new mothers how to care for their infants.

In the early 1900s, however, birth was transformed from a natural event into a technological marvel. New pain medications and medical procedures took birth into the 20th century, and childbearing moved from home to hospital. Back then, midwives practiced mainly in rural areas where doctors were unavailable, or where poorer women could not afford to deliver in a hospital.

Ironically, as these medically assisted births became more prevalent in America, professional midwifery became more regulated than it had been in the past. In the early 1920s, nurse Mary Breckenridge founded the Frontier Nursing Service in eastern Kentucky to bring medical services to people in areas too poor for hospitals, as well as to women who could not afford to have their babies delivered by a high-priced doctor. After completing her midwifery training in England, Breckenridge made prenatal care an additional focus of her service.

Midwife care around the world was proving itself to be both low in cost and high in quality. The Maternity Association and the Lobenstine Clinic (both in New York) established the first U.S. midwifery school and graduated its first class in 1933. In the mid-1930s, the Frontier Nursing Service opened its own nurse-midwifery school, and it remains today the oldest continuing U.S. midwifery program.

During the next few decades, most women who were able to deliver in a hospital preferred the lull of pain medication and the perceived safety of the medical establishment, and midwifery remained a tool of poor and rural women. Pregnancy and childbirth were considered medical procedures best left in the hands of obstetricians and gynecologists.

Since the 1950s, however, this attitude has been changing as more women insist on more natural methods of giving birth. In 1955, the American College of Nurse-Midwives (ACNM), the premier midwife organization in the United States, was established. This creation of a nationally standardized entity to regulate midwife training and practice introduced midwifery as a positive, healthy, and safe alternative to hospital births. The nurse-midwife, officially known as a certified nurse-midwife (CNM), has gradually become accepted as a respected member of the health care teams involved with family planning, pregnancy, and labor.

A number of studies have indicated that babies delivered by nurse-midwives are less likely to experience low birth weights and other health complications than babies delivered by physicians. In fact, a recent study from the National Center for Health Statistics, Centers for Disease Control and Prevention, indicates that the risk of death for the baby during birth was 33 percent lower for CNM-assisted deliveries than for physician-attended births.

The proven safety standards of births attended by nurse-midwives, the cost-effectiveness of a CNM-assisted pregnancy and labor, and the personal touch that many women get from their nurse-midwives will ensure that CNMs become vital links between traditional birthing practices and the high-tech worlds of today and tomorrow.

THE JOB

Nurse-midwives examine pregnant women and monitor the growth and development of fetuses. Typically a nurse-midwife is responsible for all phases of a normal pregnancy, including prenatal care, assisting during labor, and providing follow-up care. A nurse-midwife always works in consultation with a physician, who can be called upon should complications arise during pregnancy or childbirth. Nurse-midwives can provide emergency assistance to their patients while physicians are called. In most states, nurse-midwives are authorized to prescribe and administer medications. Many nurse-midwives provide the full spectrum of women's health care, including regular gynecological exams and well-woman care.

Not all midwives are certified nurse-midwives. Most states recognize other categories of midwives, including *direct-entry (or licensed) midwives, certified professional midwives*, and *lay (or empirical) midwives*.

Direct-entry midwives are not required to be nurses in order to practice as midwives. They typically assist in home births or at birthing centers and are trained through a combination of formal education, apprenticeship, and self-education. Direct-entry midwives are legally recognized in 29 states that offer licensing, certification, or registration programs, and they perform most of the services of CNMs. Although they generally have professional relationships with physicians, hospitals, and laboratories to provide support and emergency services, few direct-entry midwives actually practice in medical centers. Direct-entry midwives can receive the certified midwife designation from the American College of Nurse-Midwives in recognition of their professional abilities.

Certified professional midwives (CPMs) must meet the basic requirements of the North American Registry of Midwives (NARM). Potential CPMs must pass a written examination and an assessment of their skills, and they must have proven training assisting in out-of-hospital births. The NARM accepts various midwifery programs and practical apprenticeship as a basis for certification. For more information, visit http://www.narm.org.

Lay midwives usually train by apprenticing with established midwives, although some may acquire formal education as well. Lay midwives are not certified or licensed, either because they lack the necessary experience and education or because they pursue nontraditional childbirth techniques. Many lay midwives practice only as part of religious communities or specific ethnic groups, and they typically assist only in home birth situations. Some states have made it illegal for lay midwives to charge for their services.

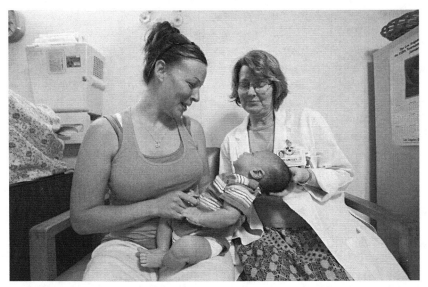

A midwife examines a seven-week-old boy. *(Jeff Adkins, AP Photo)*

Since the education and certification standards for direct-entry midwives, certified professional midwives, and lay midwives vary from state to state, the rest of this article will deal only with certified nurse-midwives, who must complete a core nursing curriculum—as well as midwifery training—to become midwives. When the terms *nurse-midwife* and *midwife* are used in this article, certified nurse-midwife is implied.

Deborah Woolley has been a registered nurse since 1975 and has been practicing as a nurse-midwife since 1983. For Woolley, midwifery offered her the opportunity to have a positive impact on women's health care and childbirth experiences. "I started out as a nurse assigned to the labor and delivery unit. But I became frustrated with the type of care the women were getting," Woolley says. "You'll find that a lot among midwives. Most of the midwives I talk to can point to an event that was the straw that broke the camel's back, as it were—when they realized that they wanted to have more influence over the experience the woman is having. Midwifery's focus is on improving conditions for women and their families. In a way, midwifery is a radical departure from the old way of looking at pregnancy."

Woolley typically arrives at the hospital at 7:00 A.M. and spends the first hour or more seeing patients in postpartum—that is, women who have given birth the day or night before. At about 8:30 A.M., Woolley goes down to the clinic to begin seeing other patients. "I work a combination of full days and half-days during the week. On a half-day, I'll see patients for four hours and work on paperwork for one hour. On a full day, I'll see patients for eight hours and work on paperwork for two hours," she says. "But that doesn't mean I always leave exactly at 5:00. At the clinic, we see everyone who shows up."

After Woolley meets a new patient, she'll spend an hour or so taking the patient's medical history, examining her, and getting her scheduled into the prenatal care system. "I also ask about a patient's life. I spend time with the patient and try to get to know her and what's going on in her life. It makes a big difference in the care she's provided. I think one of the things that makes midwives so effective is that they really get to know their patients."

An important part of a nurse-midwife's work is the education of patients. Nurse-midwives teach their patients about proper nutrition and fitness for healthy pregnancies and about different techniques for labor and delivery. Nurse-midwives also counsel their patients in the postpartum period about breast-feeding, parenting, and other areas concerning the health of mother and child. Nurse-midwives provide counseling on several other issues, including sexually transmitted diseases, spousal and child abuse, and social support networks. In some cases, this counseling may extend to family members of the soon-to-be or new mother, or even to older siblings of the family's newest addition. Woolley believes that this education is one of a midwife's key responsibilities. "I spend a lot of time teaching things like nutrition, the process of fetal development, and basic parenting skills. I'll refer patients to Lamaze classes. I'll also screen patients for family problems, such as violence in the home, and teach them how to get out of abusive situations," Woolley says. "In other words, I'll teach a patient anything she needs to know if she's pregnant. I try to empower women to take charge of their own health care and their own lives."

Apart from seeing patients, Woolley is also responsible for maintaining patient records. "I have to review lab results and ultrasounds and fill out birth certificates—things like that," she says. "There's a lot of writing involved, too. I have to document everything that I do with patients, including what I've done and how and why I've done it." This may include recording patient information, filing documents and patient charts, doing research to find out why a woman is having a particular problem, and consulting with physicians and other medical personnel. Many midwives build close relationships with their patients and try to be available for their patients at any time of the day or night.

REQUIREMENTS

High School

In high school, you should begin preparing for a career as a nurse-midwife by taking a broad range of college preparatory courses, with a focus on science classes. Anatomy, biology, and chemistry will give you solid background information for what you will be studying in college. Additional classes in sociology and psychology will help you learn how to deal with a variety of patients from different ethnic and economic groups. English and business classes will teach you how to deal with the paperwork involved in any profession. Finally, you should consider learning foreign languages if you want to serve as a midwife to immigrant communities.

Postsecondary Training

All CNMs begin their careers as registered nurses. (See the article "Registered Nurses.") After you have completed your undergraduate education and passed the licensing exam to become a registered nurse, you can apply to nurse-midwifery programs. All graduates of midwifery education programs must have a master's degree in order to be able to take the national certifying exam offered by the American Midwifery Certification Board. There are 38 nurse-midwifery education programs in the United States that are accredited by the Accreditation Commission for Midwifery Education. Graduate programs that result in master's degrees usually take 16 to 24 months to complete, and some also require one year of clinical experience in order to earn a nurse-midwife degree. In these programs, the prospective nurse-midwife is trained to provide primary care services, gynecological care, preconception and prenatal care, labor delivery and management, and postpartum and infant care. Doctorate degrees (such as a Doctor of Nursing Practice) are typically required for those who want to work in top levels of administration, in research, or in education. These degrees normally take four to five years to complete. Approximately 80 percent of CNMs have a master's degree, according to the ACNM. Five percent have a doctoral degree.

Procedures that nurse-midwives are trained to perform include physical examinations, pap smears, and episiotomies. They may also repair incisions from cesarean sections, administer anesthesia, and prescribe medications. Nurse-midwives are trained to provide counseling on subjects such as nutrition, breastfeeding, and infant care. Nurse-midwives learn to provide both physical and emotional support to pregnant women and their families.

Certification or Licensing

After earning either a midwifery certificate from a nationally accredited nurse-midwifery program or a master's degree in midwifery, midwives are required to take a national examination administered by the American Midwifery Certification Board. Upon passing the exam, the new midwife achieves full endorsement as a medical professional, as well as the title certified nurse-midwife. Those who have passed this examination are licensed to practice nurse-midwifery in all 50 states. Each state, however, has its own laws and regulations governing the activities and responsibilities of nurse-midwives.

All states and the District of Columbia require a license to practice nursing. To obtain a license, graduates of approved nursing schools must pass a national examination. Nurses may be licensed by more than one state. In some states, continuing education is a condition for license renewal. Different titles require different education and training levels.

Other Requirements

If you are interested in becoming a nurse-midwife, you will need skills that aren't necessarily taught in midwifery programs. Nurse-midwives need to enjoy working with people, learning about their patients' needs, and helping them through a very important life change. They should be sympathetic to the needs of their patients. They need to be independent and able to accept responsibility for their actions and decisions. Strong observation skills are key, as nurse-midwives must be tuned into their patients' needs during pregnancy and labor. Nurse-midwives also need to listen well and respond appropriately. They must communicate effectively with patients, family members, physicians, and other hospital staff, as well as insurance company personnel. Finally, nurse-midwives should be confident and composed, responding well in an emergency and keeping their patients calm.

EXPLORING

Volunteer work at your local hospital or clinic may put you in contact with nurse-midwives who can help you learn more about midwifery. You might also volunteer to visit and offer emotional support to laboring mothers-to-be at a hospital or freestanding birth center.

You may wish to contact a professional midwifery organization for more information about the field. These associations often publish journals or newsletters to keep members informed of new issues in midwifery. The better-known organizations may have Web sites that can give you more information about midwifery in your area. A list of some organizations is provided at the end of this article.

Finally, young women may wish to see a nurse-midwife in lieu of a physician for their well-woman care. Although nurse-midwives are usually thought of in conjunction with pregnancy, many women use nurse-midwives as their primary medical contact from their teenage years through menopause.

EMPLOYERS

There are more than 11,540 nurse-midwives in the United States. More than half work primarily in an office or clinic environment, and physician practices and hospitals are the places where most CNMs are employed. At hospitals, CNMs see patients and attend deliveries on hospital grounds and use hospital-owned equipment for examinations and other procedures. Additional medical personnel are always available for emergency situations. Other nurse-midwives work in family planning clinics and other health care clinics and privately funded agencies. These nurse-midwives usually have relationships with specific hospitals and physicians in case of an emergency. Finally, some nurse-midwives operate their own clinics and birthing centers, while others work independently and specialize in home birth deliveries.

STARTING OUT

Deborah Woolley earned a bachelor's degree in nursing and then began her career as a nurse at a labor and delivery unit in a Texas hospital. While working, she attended graduate school and earned a master's degree in maternal child nursing. She then went to Chicago, where she began training as a nurse-midwife. "After earning my nurse-midwifery degree," Woolley says, "I heard there were openings at Cook County Hospital [now called John H. Stroger Jr. Hospital of Cook County] here in Chicago. So I applied for a job there. What I liked about Cook County was that they continued to train me while I was working. They gave me assertiveness training and training in urban health issues."

Like Woolley, most nurse-midwives finish their formal education in nursing and midwifery before beginning work. They usually have some opportunities to work with patients as a student. Beginning midwives may also intern at a hospital or clinic to fulfill class requirements.

Nurse-midwives can begin their careers in various ways. Some may move from an internship to a full-time job when they complete their education requirements at a certain facility. Others may seek out a position through a professional midwifery organization or try for a job at a specific location that interests them. Finally, some nurse-midwives begin by working as nurses in other areas of health care and then move into midwifery as opportunities become available.

The American College of Nurse-Midwives offers an online career center for midwives (http://assoc.healthecareers.com/acnm/association-home) that allows job candidates to post their resumes and search job listings.

ADVANCEMENT

With experience, a nurse-midwife can advance into a supervisory role or into an administrative capacity at a hospital, family planning clinic, birthing center, or other facility. Many nurse-midwives, like Deborah Woolley, choose to continue their education and complete Ph.D. programs. With a doctorate, a nurse-midwife can do research or teaching. "I spent four-and-a-half years at Cook County while I was working on my Ph.D.," Woolley says. "From there I was recruited to Colorado to head up the midwifery unit at a hospital there. After six years as a director in Colorado, I learned that the director's position here at the University of Illinois–Chicago was open, and I jumped at the chance to come back to Chicago."

Nurse-midwives with advanced degrees may choose to move away from the day-to-day patient care and write for journals or magazines. They may also lean more toward the research aspects of prenatal care and obstetrics. Finally, nurse-midwives may prefer to apply their experience and education as a midwife toward other areas of medicine or hospital administration.

EARNINGS

Certified nurse-midwives who work for large hospitals tend to earn more than those working for small hospitals, clinics, and birthing centers. The most experienced nurse-midwives, including those in supervisory, director, and administrative positions, have the highest earnings. Salaries also vary according to the region of the country and whether the employing facility is private or public. Because of their special training, CNMs are among the higher-paying nursing professions. According to Salary.com, certified nurse-midwives earned salaries that ranged from less than $76,857 to $105,734 or more in November 2010. Median annual earnings for certified nurse-midwives were $90,231. For an example of what a nurse-midwife may earn working for the government, consider a recent job posting from the Indian Health Service for a nurse-midwife to work in Albuquerque, New Mexico. Depending on experience, the salary range was GS-11 through GS-13 (levels in the federal government's General Schedule pay scale). In 2010 the annual pay for GS-11 ranged from $50,287 to $63,571, and GS-13 ranged from $71,674 to $93,175. Nurse-midwives generally enjoy a good benefits package, although these too can vary widely depending on employer. Those working in hospitals or well-established clinics or birthing centers usually receive a full complement of benefits, including medical coverage, paid sick time, and holiday and vacation pay. They may also be able to work a more flexible schedule to accommodate family or personal obligations.

WORK ENVIRONMENT

Nurse-midwives who work in hospitals or as part of a physician's practice work indoors in clean, professional surroundings. Although most nurse-midwives perform checkups and routine visits alone with their patients, a number of other health care professionals are on hand in case the midwife has a question or needs assistance in an emergency. Nurse-midwives often consult with doctors, medical insurance representatives, and family members of their patients, as well as other midwives in order to determine the best care routine for the women they serve.

In a hospital, nurse-midwives usually wear professional clothing, a lab coat, and comfortable shoes to allow for plenty of running around during the day. They often wear hospital scrubs during delivery. In a freestanding birth center, the nurse-midwives may have a more casual dress code but still maintain a professional demeanor.

Midwives try to make their offices and birthing areas as calm and as reassuring as possible so their patients feel comfortable during checkups and delivery. Soft music may play in the background, or the waiting area may be decorated like a nursery and filled with parenting magazines.

Although most nurse-midwives work a 40-hour week, these hours may not reflect the typical nine-to-five day, since babies are delivered at all hours of the day and night. Many hospitals or clinics offer nurse-midwives a more flexible schedule in exchange for having them "on-call" for births.

Finally, although there are no gender requirements in the profession, nurse-midwifery is a field dominated by women. Approximately 98 percent of nurse-midwives in the United States are female. Women have traditionally helped each other through pregnancy and delivery. Just as women who became doctors 100 years ago had to overcome many barriers, men considering entering midwifery should be prepared for hurdles of their own.

OUTLOOK

The U.S. Department of Labor predicts that employment for all registered nurses will grow much faster than the average for all careers through 2018, and this should be especially true for specialists. As certified nurse-midwives gain a reputation as highly trained and compassionate professionals, they will become an integral part of the health care community. Currently, there are more available positions than there are nurse-midwives to fill them.

There are two factors driving the demand for nurse-midwives. The first element is the growth of interest in natural childbearing techniques among women. The number of midwife-assisted births has risen dramatically since the 1970s. Some women have been attracted to midwifery because of studies that indicate natural childbirth is more healthful for mother and child than doctor-assisted childbirth. Other women have been attracted to midwifery because it emphasizes the participation of the entire family in prenatal care and labor.

The second factor in the growing demand for nurse-midwives is economic. As society moves toward managed care programs and the health care community emphasizes cost-effectiveness, midwifery should increase in popularity. This is because the care provided by nurse-midwives costs substantially less than the care provided by obstetricians and gynecologists. If the cost advantage of midwifery continues, more insurers and health maintenance organizations will probably direct patients to nurse-midwives for care.

FOR MORE INFORMATION

For information on nursing education and careers, contact
American Association of Colleges of Nursing
One Dupont Circle, NW, Suite 530
Washington, DC 20036-1135
Tel: 202-463-6930
http://www.aacn.nche.edu

This organization is the largest and most widely known midwifery organization in the United States. The ACNM accredits midwifery programs. For more information on the career and education of nurse-midwives, visit the ACNM Web site.

American College of Nurse-Midwives (ACNM)
8403 Colesville Road, Suite 1550
Silver Spring MD 20910-6374
Tel: 240-485-1800
http://www.midwife.org

The AMCB is the national certifying body for nurse-midwives. For more information on the certification process, contact

American Midwifery Certification Board (AMCB)
849 International Drive, Suite 205
Linthicum, MD 21090-2228
Tel: 866-366-9632
http://www.accmidwife.org

The following organization can provide information about all types of midwifery:

Midwives Alliance of North America
611 Pennsylvania Avenue, SE, #1700
Washington DC 20003-4303
Tel: 888-923-6262
E-mail: info@mana.org
http://www.mana.org

Nurse Practitioners

OVERVIEW

Nurse practitioners are one of four classifications of advanced practice nurses (APNs). APNs are registered nurses who have advanced training and education. This training enables them to carry out many of the responsibilities traditionally handled by physicians. Some nurse practitioners specialize in a certain field, such as pediatrics, oncology, critical care, or primary care. The most common specialty is a family nurse practitioner who usually serves community-based health clinics. There are approximately 135,000 nurse practitioners employed in the United States.

HISTORY

Nurse practitioners first appeared on the scene following World War II, partially in response to the acute shortage of physicians. In addition, there was an influx of former corpsmen who hoped to utilize their military training and experience to fill the void of medical practitioners.

Even prior to the establishment of the first training program for nurse practitioners at the University of Colorado in 1965, nurses had performed simple but time-consuming tasks formerly regarded as the physician's responsibility, such as taking blood pressures or administering intravenous feedings or medications. Those involved in the first nurse practitioner training program at the University of Colorado believed that nurse practitioners could perform many of the time-consuming tasks then restricted to physicians, thus freeing up the physicians to handle more complex cases.

The nurse practitioner has also fulfilled a need to focus more on health maintenance and illness prevention. In 1986, a study carried out by the U.S. Congress Office of Technology Assessment found that "within their areas of competence, nurse practitioners provide care whose quality is equivalent to that of care provided by physicians." In preventive care and communication with patients, nurse practitioners were found to outperform doctors. Nurse practitioners are assuming an increasingly important role in the health care industry.

THE JOB

A nurse practitioner's responsibilities depend on the work setting and area of specialization. A nurse practitioner may work in close collaboration with a physician at a hospital, health center, or private practice office. Sometimes, as in the case of rural health care providers, they may have only weekly telephone contact with a physician. In all states, a nurse practitioner may write prescriptions, but a physician's signature is often required to validate the prescription.

Family nurse practitioners are often based in community health clinics. They provide primary care to people of all ages, assessing, diagnosing, and treating common illnesses and injuries. Their interactions with patients have a strong emphasis on teaching and counseling for health maintenance. Nurse practitioners recognize the importance of the social and emotional aspects of health care in addition to the more obvious physical factors.

Nurse practitioners in other specialties perform similar tasks, although they may work with different age groups or with people in schools or institutional settings. Just as physicians do, nurse practitioners select a field of specialization. A *pediatric nurse practitioner* provides primary health care for infants through adolescents. *Gerontological nurse practitioners* are often based in nursing homes and work with older adults. *School nurse practitioners* work in school settings and provide primary health care for students. *Occupational health nurse practitioners* focus on employment-related health problems and injuries. *Psychiatric nurse practitioners* work with people who have mental or emotional problems. *Women's health care nurse practitioners* provide primary care for women from adolescence through old age and may provide services from contraception to hormone replacement therapy.

Nurse practitioners also practice in the following subspecialty areas: allergy and immunology, cardiovascular, dermatology, emergency care, endocrinology, gastroenterology, hematology and oncology, neurology, occupational health, orthopedics, pulmonology and respiratory, sports medicine, and urology.

REQUIREMENTS

High School

If you want to become a nurse practitioner, you will first need to become a registered nurse. (See the article "Registered Nurses.") To prepare for this career, you should take high school mathematics and science courses, including biology, chemistry, and physics. Health courses will also be helpful. English and speech courses should not be neglected because you must be able to communicate well with patients.

Postsecondary Training

You must be a registered nurse (RN) before you can become a nurse practitioner. There are three basic kinds of training programs that you may choose from to become a registered nurse: associate's degree, diploma, and bachelor's degree. Which of the three training programs to choose depends on your career goals. A bachelor's degree in nursing is required for most supervisory or administrative positions, for jobs in public health agencies, and for admission to graduate nursing programs. A master's degree is usually necessary to prepare for a nursing specialty or to teach. For some specialties, such as nursing research, a Ph.D. is essential.

A master's degree is required to become a nurse practitioner. Admission to quality nurse practitioner programs is very competitive. Nurse practitioner programs last one to two years and provide advanced study in diagnostic skills, health assessment, pharmacology, clinical management, and research skills. Usually the student begins with generalist work and later focuses on a specific nurse practitioner specialty.

Certification or Licensing

Not all states require nurse practitioners to be nationally certified; however, certification is strongly recommended by those in the profession. Certification in a variety of specialties is offered by such organizations as the American Nurses Association, the American Academy of Nurse Practitioners, the Oncology Nursing Certification Corporation, the Pediatric Nursing Certification Board, and the Society of Urologic Nurses and Associates. Certification typically involves passing a written exam, and requirements

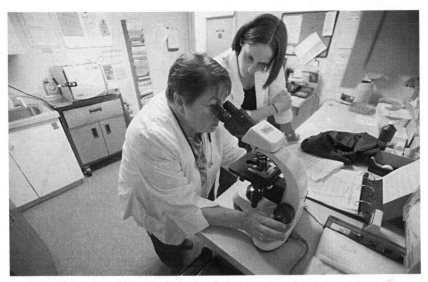

A nurse practitioner (*left*) and a physician assistant work in a laboratory. *(Charlie Neibergall, AP Photo)*

for recertification usually include completing a certain amount of continuing education. Exact requirements vary according to the certifying group.

All states and the District of Columbia require a license to practice nursing. To obtain a license, graduates of approved nursing schools must pass a national examination. Nurses may be licensed by more than one state. In some states, continuing education is a condition for license renewal.

State requirements for licensing and registration of nurse practitioners vary. All states license them to prescribe medications independently, although some states have restrictions regarding the prescription of controlled substances. For specifics, contact your state's nursing board. (See the National Council of State Boards of Nursing Web site at https://www.ncsbn.org for contact information.)

Other Requirements

To be a good nurse practitioner you should enjoy working with people and be strongly committed to making a positive difference in people's lives. You must develop excellent communication skills and should have patience, flexibility, and the ability to remain calm in an emergency. Since you may work independently much of the time, you need to be able to take active responsibility in health care situations and have good judgment regarding these situations. Your role will be strongly focused on health maintenance and prevention, so you should enjoy teaching and counseling as well.

EXPLORING

The Internet is a helpful research tool to learn more about nursing careers. Visit the Web sites of nursing programs and professional associations for tips on planning your education and career goals. (See the end of the article for contact information.) In addition to your research, talk to people about your interest in nursing. Your school's career counselor can give you advice on picking a nursing program and may even help you find contacts in the medical field. Visit a local hospital or other medical facility and ask if you can speak to a member of the nursing staff about his or her career. If the facility accepts volunteers, don't hesitate to sign up. Hands-on experience is the number one way to explore a career in health care.

EMPLOYERS

Approximately 135,000 nurse practitioners are employed in the United States. They work in hospitals, clinics, physicians' offices, community health centers, rural health clinics, nursing homes, mental health centers, educational institutions, student health centers, nursing schools, home health agencies, hospices, prisons, industrial organizations, the U.S. military, and other health care settings. In the states that allow nurse practitioners to practice independently, self-employment is an option.

The particular specialty a nurse practitioner pursues obviously is a major factor in determining their employment setting. Another important factor is the degree of autonomy they desire. Nurse practitioners in remote rural areas have the most autonomy, but they must be willing to spend a lot of time on the road visiting patients who are unable to get to the clinic, to be on call at all hours, and to make do with less than optimal facilities and equipment.

STARTING OUT

The career services office of your nursing school is a good place to begin the employment search. Contacts you have made in clinical settings during your nurse practitioner program are also useful sources of information on job opportunities. Nursing registries, nurse employment services, and your state employment office have information about available jobs. Nursing journals and newspapers list openings. If you are interested in working for the federal government, contact the Office of Personnel Management for your region. Applying directly to hospitals, nursing homes, and other health care agencies is also an option for nurse practitioners.

ADVANCEMENT

Nurse practitioners have many avenues for advancement. After gaining experience, they may move into positions that offer more responsibility and higher salaries. Some choose to move into administrative or supervisory positions in health care organizations or nursing schools. They may become faculty members at nursing schools or directors of nursing at hospitals, clinics, or other health agencies.

Some advance by doing additional academic and clinical study that gives them certification in specialized fields. Those with an interest in research, teaching, consulting, or policy making in the nursing field would do well to consider earning a Ph.D. in nursing.

EARNINGS

Geographic location, experience, and specialty area of practice are all factors that influence salary levels for nurse practitioners. The American Academy of Nurse Practitioners reports average base salary for full-time nurse practitioners was $89,450 in 2009. According to the 2009 National Salary Survey done by *Advance for Nurse Practitioners*, a news magazine for nurse practitioners, the average salary for nurse practitioners (all specialties) was $89,579. Details of the survey show that average salaries vary by specialties and settings. For example, nurse practitioners working in emergency care earned on average $105,152, and those specializing in mental health medicine earned $100,140 annually. At the other end of the pay scale, however, were nurse practitioners working in college health, who averaged $81,981, and those in elementary and secondary school settings, who averaged $76,965 annually. Some practitioners earned even more than this amount, with salaries in the $120,000s.

Full-time nurse practitioners' benefits may vary by employer. For example, those in their own practices must provide their own retirement plans. Generally, though, nurse practitioners employed by hospitals, clinics, and schools receive health insurance, paid vacation and sick days, and retirement plans. Some employers also pay for continuing education.

WORK ENVIRONMENT

The work environment depends on the nurse practitioner's specialty. Some work in remote, rural settings in small, local health care clinics. Others work in modern hospitals or nursing homes. Some nurse practitioners may work with patients who are fearful of any type of health care provider or who may have never been to a clinic before. Some patients may resent being seen by "just a nurse" instead of the doctor. Others may work with medical staff who are uncooperative and who feel threatened by the role of the nurse practitioner. All of these situations require tact, patience, and maturity. Nurse practitioners must often work long hours.

OUTLOOK

The U.S. Department of Labor predicts that employment for registered nurses will grow much faster than the average for all careers through 2018, and the job outlook for nurse practitioners is especially strong. One reason for this is that the nurse practitioner is increasingly being recognized as a provider of the high-quality—yet cost-effective—medical care that the nation's health care system needs. In addition, more and more people are recognizing the importance of preventive health care, which is one of the nurse practitioner's greatest strengths. There should be an especially strong demand for gerontological nurse practitioners as the percentage of the U.S population in the over-65 age group increases.

Nurse practitioner organizations are working to promote legislation that will increase the degree of autonomy available to nurse practitioners and make it easier for them to receive insurance company reimbursement. This should make the profession an even more attractive advancement route for RNs.

FOR MORE INFORMATION

The following organizations provide information on nurse practitioner careers:

American Academy of Nurse Practitioners
PO Box 12846
Austin, TX 78711-2846
Tel: 512-442-4262
E-mail: admin@aanp.org
http://www.aanp.org

American College of Nurse Practitioners
1501 Wilson Boulevard, Suite 509
Arlington, VA 22209-2403
Tel: 703-740-2529
E-mail: acnp@acnpweb.org
http://www.acnpweb.org

Gerontological Advanced Practice Nurses Association
East Holly Avenue, Box 56
Pitman, NJ 08071-0056
Tel: 866-355-1392
E-mail: GAPNA@ajj.com
https://www.gapna.org

National Association of Nurse Practitioners in Women's Health
505 C Street, NE
Washington, DC 20002-5809
Tel: 202-543-9693
E-mail: info@npwh.org
http://www.npwh.org

National Association of Pediatric Nurse Practitioners
20 Brace Road, Suite 200
Cherry Hill, NJ 08034-2634
Tel: 856-857-9700
E-mail: info@napnap.org
http://www.napnap.org

This Web site offers information on issues affecting nursing practitioners in all specialties and provides links to other sites of interest.
Advance for Nurse Practitioners and Physician Assistants
http://nurse-practitioners-and-physician-assistants.advanceweb
.com/Default.aspx

Nursing Home Administrators

QUICK FACTS

School Subjects
Business
Sociology

Personal Skills
Communication/ideas
Leadership/management

Work Environment
Primarily indoors
Primarily one location

Minimum Education Level
Bachelor's degree

Salary Range
$49,750 to $81,850 to
$140,300+

Certification or Licensing
Recommended (certification)
Required (licensing)

Outlook
Faster than the average

DOT
187

GOE
14.01.01

NOC
0311

O*NET-SOC
11-9111.00

OVERVIEW

Nursing home administrators manage nursing homes. Their duties are wide ranging, covering everything from keeping track of financial accounts to making sure the facility is up to code to greeting residents at social events. In addition, administrators supervise managers throughout the residence. *Nursing home managers* head different departments of a facility, such as housekeeping, dietary, or human resources, and they report any problems or needs to the nursing home administrator, who then addresses the situation. Administrators work closely with the medical director and nursing staff to ensure proper medical treatment for all residents. They also act as the nursing home's representative during interactions with residents' families, government agencies, and the community.

HISTORY

Institutions for the elderly have not always been clean and cheery places. Nevertheless, such institutions have existed in the United States since colonial times. One such institution was the poor house, modeled after the English almshouse. Elderly people without means of support or families to care for them often ended up living their final days in these dismal places. Religious institutions, such as convents, also offered places for the old and sick to stay. And, of course, families provided care for their senior members, often with several generations living in one household.

Nursing Home Facts

- There are 16,100 certified nursing homes in the United States.
- More than 1.7 million people live in nursing homes.
- The average age of an individual who enters a nursing home is 79.
- Twelve million older Americans are expected to need long-term care services and support by 2020.

Source: American Association of Homes and Services for the Aging

It was not until the 20th century, however, that the long-term care of seniors became organized into a business. According to the American Health Care Association, the first nursing homes in the United States came into existence around 1900. Originally these homes were boarding houses, places where people paid rent that covered rooms and meals. As boarding house residents aged, some became physically unable to care for themselves and needed help with everyday activities. In addition, those without other family members, who otherwise would take care of them, sought places that offered basic medical care in addition to meals and lodging. Boarding house owners recognized the need to provide housing and medical services for these older residents. Those who began to supply these services became the first people to run nursing homes and were, essentially, the first nursing home administrators.

By 1920, state health departments developed licensure programs for nursing homes within their jurisdiction to better regulate facilities and their services. The 1930s saw the development of the Social Security and Old Age Assistance programs, government programs designed to give the elderly financial support that they could use for their care. In 1965 the programs Medicare and Medicaid were added to the Social Security Act. These two programs paid providers of care services directly and helped to spur the growth of the long-term care industry.

Today, as the country's senior population expands, as medical and technological advances are made, and as lifestyles change, the need for well-managed, comfortable, clean, and affordable long-term care for the elderly is greater than ever.

THE JOB

The term nursing home usually makes people think of what are called skilled nursing facilities. These facilities provide 24-hour nursing care, meals, and living space to residents. Many nursing home administrators work at skilled nursing facilities. However, other types of nursing or care facilities also exist. For example, intermediate-care facilities, which provide residents with meals and shelter and may also provide regular medical care, although not on a 24-hour basis, employ administrators. And administrators work at residential care facilities, also called assisted living facilities. These facilities provide residents with meals and living space but offer only limited medical supervision and care.

In addition to these three distinctions (skilled nursing, intermediate care, and residential care facilities), nursing homes can also be grouped into three categories based on their ownership. Not-for-profit nursing homes are run by voluntary organizations, such as fraternal or religious groups. Proprietary facilities are those run for profit by individuals, partnerships, or corporations. And government facilities are run, of course, by the government and include such places as veterans' homes and state-run nursing homes.

However, no matter what type of facility they work for and no matter who owns the facility, all nursing home administrators are responsible for every aspect of maintaining and operating that home. Their many duties range from management of personnel to public relations. Depending on the size of the facility, administrators may have one or more assistants to help with the daily responsibilities.

If the nursing home is part of a large corporation, the administrator must meet with the governing board or other administrators from different facilities within the company. They take an active role in helping plan budgets and programs. For example, if staff resources are low or new equipment or remodeling is needed, the administrator must explain the situation to the corporate office in order to get proper funding for the project. They may also help set fee schedules for patient services.

Administrators oversee every department in the nursing home from dietary to medical records. Some departments may have their own managers, but these managers must report to the administrator. Many times, administrators interview and hire department managers; they also have a voice in how staff members are trained and supervised. Administrators also work with the medical director and nursing director to plan medical policies and procedures that will ensure the best health care for all the residents. They also work with the activities director in planning recreational events, holiday parties, and other year-round entertainment for the residents.

Administrators are responsible for dealing with different government agencies that monitor health care. Nursing homes must meet strict guidelines before becoming Medicare and/or Medicaid certified by the federal agency Centers for Medicare and Medicaid Services (CMS). Without CMS approval, Medicare and Medicaid will not pay for any services rendered at the facility. In addition, every nursing home facility undergoes an annual inspection by the state's health department. Any discrepancies or violations found are directed to the administrator for explanation. Many nursing homes also participate in voluntary quality assurance programs that measure the performance of the facility and its staff.

If there are problems with the staff, or complaints regarding a client's treatment or well-being, the administrator must intervene. A good administrator should be able to listen, assess the situation, and act accordingly. Administrators should not only be visible to patients and their families, but be approachable as well.

REQUIREMENTS

High School

Are you thinking about a career in health administration? If you are, you should know that there are several key classes to include in your high school curriculum. Managing a nursing home is very similar to managing a business. Classes such as accounting, business management, and computer science will help prepare you for the business side of this job. Quantitative skills are needed to excel in this career, so make sure you take as many math classes as possible. Science and health classes are important to take and will prepare you for college. High school classes in sociology, psychology, and social studies can provide you with a background for understanding a variety of people. And, because you will be working with so many different people and must give directions, take English, speech, and foreign language classes to hone your communication and leadership skills.

Postsecondary Training

Most nursing home administrators have a college degree in health administration, business, human resources, or another related field. A few states do allow licensing for administrators who hold an associate's degree and have a certain amount of experience. It is recommended, however, that you get a bachelor's degree. One reason for this is that requirements for professional certification stipulate that anyone licensed must also hold a bachelor's degree to be eligible for certification. In addition, most employers insist on hiring only those with at least a bachelor's degree.

Many colleges and universities across the United States offer bachelor's degrees in health care administration, health service administration, or long-term care administration with concentrations or minors in nursing home management. The Association of University Programs in Health Administration certifies undergraduate and graduate programs that meet the organization's standards. The National Association of Long Term Care Administrator Boards grants academic approval to undergraduate programs in long-term care administration. The Commission on Accreditation of Healthcare Management Education is the accrediting body for graduate programs in health administration education. Graduates of advanced-degree programs usually have a master's of science in health administration or a master's in business administration in health care management.

Courses you are likely to take as an undergraduate cover subjects such as health law, gerontology, medical terminology, and health care financial management. In addition, expect to take classes such as accounting, marketing, computer science, and organizational theory. Some programs also require students to complete an internship, also called an administrator-in-training program.

Certification or Licensing

Professional certification is available from the American College of Health Care Administrators. Certification requirements include having a bachelor's degree, having two years of professional experience as a nursing home administrator, completing a certain amount of continuing education, and passing the certification exam. Candidates who meet all requirements receive the designation certified nursing home administrator. The certified assisted living administrator designation is also available. Certification demonstrates an administrator's level of experience and professionalism and is recommended. The American College of Healthcare Executives (ACHE) offers the certified healthcare executive designation to candidates who pass an examination and meet other requirements. Fellow status is available to certified healthcare executives with advanced experience and skills. Contact the ACHE for more information.

All nursing home administrators must be licensed. All states and the District of Columbia require candidates to pass a national licensing exam given by the National Association of Long Term Care Administrator Boards. In addition, many states require candidates to pass a state exam as well as to fulfill certain requirements, such as having completed an administrator-in-training program of a certain length and completing a certain number of continuing education hours. Since these state requirements vary, you will need to check with the licensing board of the state in which you hope to work for specific information.

Other Requirements

Nursing home administrators must have a keen sense for business and enjoy managing people, budgets, and resources. They should be able to work well with a wide variety of people, from government officials to residents' families. But just as important as having a feel for business, nursing home administrators must have a special interest in helping people, especially the elderly. Administrators need to be aware of the emotional and physical challenges their residents face and be able to figure out ways to make their facilities accommodating. Administrators need to have a positive attitude and to be committed to lifelong learning, since continuing education is an essential part of this work.

EXPLORING

To explore the field of nursing home administration, try contacting a nursing home in your area and make an appointment to speak with the administrator or assistant administrator about this work. They should be able to answer any questions you may have about the job, as well as give you a feel for their workday.

Hands-on experience is also important, so volunteer at a local nursing home or assisted living residence. You can help conduct activities such as games, arts and crafts, holiday celebrations, reading aloud to the sight impaired, or simply keeping lonely seniors company. Most, if not all, facilities welcome volunteers. In addition, there may be opportunities for paid part-time or summer jobs at these facilities. Even if you end up only working in the kitchen, you will still get a good feel for the structure of the business.

EMPLOYERS

There are about 16,000 certified nursing homes located throughout the United States. Each nursing home, depending on its size, needs administrators and assistant administrators to oversee its operation. Nonprofit groups, corporations, and government agencies employ administrators in a variety of settings: at skilled nursing, intermediate care, and residential facilities. No matter what the facility is, however, each needs administrative leadership to ensure successful operation.

Job opportunities vary from state to state. According to the Administration on Aging, California had the largest number of residents age 65 and over in 2008, with approximately 4.1 million. Other states with large populations of elderly people were Florida (3.2 million), New York (2.6 million), Texas (2.5 million), and Pennsylvania (1.9 million). Alaska, on the other hand, ranked at the bottom with approximately 50,277 residents in this age group. It makes sense to conclude that opportunities for nursing home employment are most plentiful in areas with high concentrations of older residents.

STARTING OUT

A nursing home administrator is considered a high executive position, so it is quite rare to land this job directly after graduation. Working as an assistant administrator is a more realistic mid-level management position. It is not uncommon for administrators to have one or more assistants responsible for different aspects of running the nursing home, especially at larger facilities. For example, one assistant administrator may be in charge of human resources and benefits, while another is assigned to keeping inventory and purchasing supplies. The administrator oversees the work of each assistant.

As a starting point for the career of administrator, however, you may begin as an activity director or, depending on the size of the facility, as an assistant to the activity director. Nursing home patients look forward to a variety of diversions to help make their stay pleasant and enjoyable. Coordinating weekly patient entertainment, such as bingo, arts and crafts, holiday parties, and other celebrations, are some of the duties of an activity director.

Other routes into this field include jobs that familiarize you with government agencies and case management.

ADVANCEMENT

It is hard to identify a typical route of advancement for the nursing home administrator, since this is already considered an executive position. Experienced administrators might choose to work for a larger nursing home with a bigger staff. If employed by a chain, administrators may advance by being transferred to other nursing home locations or promoted to the corporate office. Administrative positions at hospitals, health maintenance organizations, pharmaceutical companies, or national associations, such as the Red Cross, are other options for advancement. The skills and experience nursing home administrators possess, such as management and budgeting, can be easily applied to other areas of the corporate world.

EARNINGS

The U.S. Department of Labor (DOL) reports that medical and health services managers working at nursing care facilities earned mean annual salaries of $81,850 in 2009. Salaries for all medical and health services managers ranged from less than $49,750 to $140,300 or more. These salaries do not include bonuses. Income also depends on the administrator's experience, the size of the facility, its ownership, and its location.

Administrators receive added benefits such as health and life insurance, paid vacation and sick time, and retirement plans.

WORK ENVIRONMENT

Most administrators are scheduled for eight-hour workdays, although they often work longer hours, especially when there are a large number of admissions or if there is a problem that needs to be addressed. Administrators must be available at all hours to handle any emergency that may arise. Most keep a regular Monday through Friday work schedule; some work on weekends.

Administrators usually have private offices, but the nature of their job takes them to every department and floor of the nursing home facility. If there is a problem in the dietary department, the administrator must go to the dietitian's office or the kitchen. A resident's complaint may take the administrator to that particular room.

Most nursing home facilities do not enforce a dress code for non-medical staff. However, it is important to dress professionally and in a manner appropriate to the environment.

OUTLOOK

Nursing home administration, like many careers in geriatric care, is a field to watch. Employment of health service managers is expected to grow faster than the average for all careers through 2018, according to the DOL. Much of the anticipated employment opportunities will be at nursing homes and other residential facilities.

One reason for this demand will be the increased number of seniors. The Administration on Aging projects there will be approximately 71.5 million older persons, age 65 years or older, by 2030. This age group will grow dramatically as more of the baby boom generation (those born from the mid-1940s to the mid-1960s) reach senior status.

People are also living longer than ever before due to improvements in medical care and healthier lifestyles. As life expectancies rise, many families are presented with the unique situation of caring for their elderly parents, and sometimes their grandparents, while raising their own young families.

Another reason nursing home facilities and those who work in them will be in demand is our mobile society. People relocate today much more than in generations past, often moving away from their original homes for better employment opportunities. It is not uncommon for the elderly to have no immediate family members living close by. The primary reason many senior citizens enter nursing homes is their inability to care for themselves due to chronic illness or advanced age. According to a study conducted by Columbia University's College of Physicians and Surgeons, the "typical" nursing home resident's stay is two and a half years. As the number of people requiring round-the-clock medical attention increases, so will the need for more nursing home facilities. This, in turn, will fuel a demand for qualified nursing home administrators.

FOR MORE INFORMATION

For information regarding nonprofit facilities, contact
American Association of Homes and Services for the Aging
2519 Connecticut Avenue, NW
Washington, DC 20008-1520
Tel: 202-783-2242
E-mail: info@aahsa.org
http://www.aahsa.org

For information on careers, certification, and licensure, contact the following organizations:
American College of Health Care Administrators
1321 Duke Street, Suite 400
Alexandria, VA 22314-3563
Tel: 202-536-5120
http://www.achca.org

American College of Healthcare Executives
One North Franklin Street, Suite 1700
Chicago, IL 60606-3529
Tel: 312-424-2800
http://www.ache.org

For information regarding long-term health care and its facilities in the United States, contact
American Health Care Association
1201 L Street, NW
Washington, DC 20005-4024
Tel: 202-842-4444
http://www.ahca.org

Contact the AUPHA for information regarding accredited academic programs in health administration.
Association of University Programs in Health Administration (AUPHA)
2000 North 14th Street, Suite 780
Arlington, VA 22201-2543
Tel: 703-894-0940
E-mail: aupha@aupha.org
http://www.aupha.org

For information on graduate programs in health administration education, contact
Commission on Accreditation of Healthcare Management Education
2111 Wilson Boulevard, Suite 700
Arlington, VA 22201-3052
Tel: 703-351-5010
E-mail: info@cahme.org
http://www.cahme.org

For information on licensing and undergraduate degree programs in long-term care administration, visit the association's Web site.
National Association of Long Term Care Administrator Boards
1444 I Street, NW, Suite 700
Washington, DC 20005-6542
Tel: 202-712-9040
E-mail: nab@nabweb.org
http://www.nabweb.org

For information on education and licensing, visit
Long Term Care Education
706 Greenwood Road
Chapel Hill, NC 27514-5923
Tel: 919-815-0387
http://www.longtermcareeducation.com

For information on a career as a health care executive, visit
**Make a Difference . . . Discover a Career in Healthcare
Management**
http://www.healthmanagementcareers.com

Nursing Instructors

OVERVIEW

Nursing instructors teach patient care to nursing students in classroom and clinical settings. They demonstrate care methods and monitor hands-on learning by their students. They instruct students in the principles and applications of biological and psychological subjects related to nursing. Some nursing instructors specialize in teaching specific areas of nursing such as surgical or oncological nursing.

Nursing instructors may be full professors, assistant professors, instructors, or lecturers, depending on their education and the facilities' nursing programs. There are approximately 55,100 nursing instructors employed in the United States.

HISTORY

In 1873, the first school of nursing in the United States was founded in Boston. In 1938, New York State passed the first law requiring that practical nurses be licensed. Even though the first school for the training of practical nurses had started almost 65 years before, and the establishment of other schools followed, the training programs lacked uniformity.

Shortly after licensure requirements surfaced, a movement toward organized training programs began that would help to ensure quality standards in the field. The role and training of the nurse have undergone radical changes since the first nursing schools were opened.

Education standards for nurses have been improving constantly since that time. Nurses are now required by all states to

QUICK FACTS

School Subjects
Biology
Chemistry
Health

Personal Skills
Helping/teaching
Technical/scientific

Work Environment
Primarily indoors
Primarily multiple locations

Minimum Education Level
Bachelor's degree

Salary Range
$38,200 to $61,360 to
$99,220+

Certification or Licensing
Voluntary (certification)
Required by all states
(licensing)

Outlook
Much faster than the average

DOT
075

GOE
12.03.02

NOC
4131

O*NET-SOC
25-1072.00

be appropriately educated and licensed to practice. Extended programs of training are offered throughout the country. The field of nursing serves an important role as a part of the health care system.

According to the American Association of Colleges of Nursing (AACN), the field of nursing is the nation's largest health care profession, and nursing students account for more than half of all health profession students in the United States.

THE JOB

Nursing instructors teach in colleges and universities or nursing schools. They teach in classrooms and in clinical settings. Their duties depend on the facility, the nursing program, and the instructor's education level. Some nursing instructors specialize in specific subjects such as chemistry or anatomy, or in a type of nursing activity such as pediatric nursing.

Many health care facilities partner with area nursing programs, so the students can actually practice what they are learning under the supervision of nursing staff and instructors. For example, the students may spend time in a hospital environment learning pediatrics and surgical care and additional time in a nursing home setting learning the health care needs of the elderly and disabled. Classroom instruction and clinical training depend on the nursing program and the degree conferred.

Mary Bell, a registered nurse who has 12 years of nursing experience, taught classes part time as an associate professor in Indiana. Classroom teaching and clinical practice were her responsibilities.

Bell says, "As part of the clinical instruction, students conferred with me regarding the patients. They assessed the patients and learned how to chart information and statistics. Sometimes their patient observations were very keen.

"I loved the clinical part of teaching," she says. "The students often brought a new perspective to nursing. They were always eager to learn and to share what they learned.

"Nursing technology and care is always changing, and the instructor shouldn't mind being challenged," states Bell. She goes on to say that the instructor must be able to create dialogue so there is an exchange of information and ideas. "It is a process between student and teacher," she observes.

Nursing instructors must spend a lot of preparation time outside the classroom and clinical setting, according to Bell. For example, the instructor must work with head nurses or charge nurses to determine the students' patient assignments. They must review patients' charts and be well informed about their current conditions prior to the student nurses appearing for their clinical instruction. Plus, there are the usual teaching responsibilities such as course planning, paper grading, and test preparation. Involvement often extends beyond the classroom.

"Professors at universities and colleges are expected to be involved with the community," says Bell. They may be required to speak to community groups or consult with businesses, and they are encouraged to be active in professional associations and on academic committees.

"In addition, many larger institutions expect professors to do research and be published in nursing or medical journals," Bell notes.

Teaching load and research requirements vary by institution and program. Full professors usually spend more of their time conducting research and publishing than assistant professors, instructors, and lecturers.

Often nursing instructors actively work in the nursing field along with teaching. "They will do this to maintain current hands-on experience and to advance their careers," Bell acknowledges. "It is a huge commitment."

"But," she adds, "it's great being able to see the light bulb turn on in the students' heads."

Top Employers and Mean Earnings, 2009

Employer	# Employed	Mean Earnings
General medical and surgical hospitals	3,480	$76,140
Business schools and computer and management training	280	$70,930
Colleges, universities, and professional schools	23,650	$65,790
Junior colleges	18,480	$62,620
Technical and trade schools	2,570	$61,820

Source: U.S. Department of Labor

REQUIREMENTS

High School

If you are interested in becoming a nursing instructor, take classes in health and the sciences to prepare for a medical career. Since nursing instructors begin as nurses themselves, you need to take classes that will prepare you for nursing programs. Talk to your school counselor about course requirements for specific programs, but plan on taking biology, chemistry, mathematics, and English courses to help build the strong foundation necessary for nursing school.

Postsecondary Training

Most nursing instructors first work as registered nurses and, therefore, have completed either a two-year associate's degree program, a three-year diploma program, or a four-year bachelor's degree program in nursing. Which of the three training programs to choose depends on your career goals. As a nurse, you should also have considerable clinical nursing experience before considering teaching.

Most universities and colleges require that their full-time professors have doctoral degrees, but many hire master's degree holders for part-time and temporary teaching positions. Two-year colleges may hire full-time teachers who have master's degrees. Smaller institutions or nursing schools may hire part-time nursing instructors who have a bachelor's degree.

Certification or Licensing

Nurses can receive voluntary certification from a variety of nursing associations. In order to practice as a registered nurse, you first must become licensed in the state in which you plan to work. Licensed RNs must graduate from an accredited school of nursing and pass a national examination. In order to renew their license, RNs must show proof of continued education and pass renewal exams. Most states honor licenses granted in other states, as long as scores are acceptable.

Other Requirements

In order to succeed as a nursing instructor, you must enjoy teaching and nursing. You should have excellent organizational and leadership skills and be able to communicate well with professional staff and students of all ages. You should be able to demonstrate skilled nursing techniques. Since you will be responsible for all the care your students administer to patients, you must have good supervision

A nursing instructor uses a tomato to demonstrate how to give an injection. *(Nikki Carlson,* Havre Daily News/*AP Photo)*

skills. In addition, you should be able to teach your students the humane side of nursing that is so important in patient and nurse relationships. New medical technologies, patient treatments, and medications are constantly being developed, so nursing instructors must stay abreast of new information in the medical field. They need to be up-to-date on the use of new medical equipment that is used for patient care.

EXPLORING

While in high school, you can explore your interest in the nursing field in a number of ways. Consult your high school counselor, school nurse, and local community nurses for information. A visit to a hospital or nursing clinic can give you a chance to observe the roles and duties of nurses in the facility and may give you the opportunity to talk one-on-one with staff members. Check to see if you can volunteer to work in a hospital, nursing home, or clinic after school, on weekends, or during summer vacation to further explore your interest.

To get a better sense of the teaching work involved in being a nursing instructor, explore your interest and talents as a teacher. Spend some time with one of your teachers after school, and ask to look at lecture notes and record-keeping procedures. Ask your teacher about the amount of work that goes into preparing a class or directing an extracurricular activity. To get some firsthand teaching experience, volunteer for a peer-tutoring program.

Visit Nursing World (http://www.nursingworld.org), Discover Nursing (http://www.discovernursing.com), and other nursing-related Web sites to keep up-to-date in this field.

EMPLOYERS

Approximately 55,100 nursing instructors are employed in the United States. They work in hospitals, clinics, colleges, and universities that offer nursing education programs. Instructors' jobs can vary greatly, depending on the employer. Many nursing instructors associated with hospitals or medical clinics work in the nursing field in addition to teaching. Those employed by large universities and colleges are more focused on academia, conducting medical research and writing medical reports of their findings.

STARTING OUT

Because you should first obtain practical experience in this field, begin by becoming a registered nurse. After graduating from an approved nursing program and passing licensure examinations, you can apply directly to hospitals, nursing homes, companies, and government agencies for employment. Jobs can also be obtained through school career services offices, employment agencies specializing in placement of nursing personnel, or through states' employment offices. Other sources of jobs include nurses' associations, professional journals, and newspaper want ads.

ADVANCEMENT

In hospitals and clinics, nursing instructors generally advance by moving up in staff ranks. Positions with higher levels of authority, and hence higher pay, include advanced practice nurses, nurse supervisors or managers, or medical administrators.

Those who work in nursing schools, colleges, or universities may advance through the academic ranks from a part-time adjunct to a full-time instructor to assistant professor to associate professor, and finally to full professor. From there, those interested in administration may become deans or directors of nursing programs. As professors advance in their careers, they frequently spend less time in the classroom and more time conducting research, public speaking, and writing.

EARNINGS

Educational background, experience, responsibilities, geographic location, and the hiring institution are factors influencing the earnings of nursing instructors.

According to the U.S. Department of Labor (DOL), nursing instructors and teachers had median annual earnings of $61,360 in 2009. Ten percent earned less than $38,200 annually, and 10 percent earned more than $99,220 annually. Full-time faculty typically receive such benefits as health insurance, retirement plans, paid sick leave, and, in some cases, funds for work-related expenses such as educational conferences.

WORK ENVIRONMENT

Nursing instructors work in colleges, universities, or nursing schools. Their clinical instruction can take place in any number of health care facilities including doctors' offices, medical clinics, hospitals, institutions, and nursing homes. Most health care environments are clean and well lighted. Inner-city facilities may be in less than desirable locations, and safety may be an issue.

All health-related careers have some health and disease risks; however, adherence to health and safety guidelines greatly minimizes the chance of contracting infectious diseases such as hepatitis and AIDS. Medical knowledge and good safety measures are also needed to limit exposure to toxic chemicals, radiation, and other hazards.

OUTLOOK

The DOL predicts that employment for registered nurses will grow much faster than the average for all occupations through 2018. In addition, those practicing in nursing specialties will also be in great demand. Because of this, there will be a corresponding demand for nursing instructors.

Several factors are fueling this shortage. There is an ongoing shortage of nursing instructors due to a declining interest by nurses in pursuing careers as educators. The AACN reports that nearly 55,000 qualified applicants to baccalaureate and graduate nursing programs were not accepted in 2009. Nearly two-thirds of responding schools said that an insufficient number of faculty members was a factor for not accepting all applicants. As more students apply to nursing school, more nursing instructors will be needed to teach students and make up for staffing shortages.

Nursing educators earn much lower salaries than those paid to nurses in clinical settings, which has reduced interest in the field. Additionally, the average age of doctorally prepared nursing professors was 56.6 years in 2002–03, according to the American Association of Colleges of Nursing. This means that during the next decade a large percentage of nursing school professors will retire. Their replacements, naturally, are drawn from the instructor ranks, and this should also add to a shortage of and demand for nursing teachers.

A lack of classroom space and clinical training sites, also highly sought after due to the emphasis on community-based services, also has limited the number of nursing educators.

FOR MORE INFORMATION

For more information on nursing and becoming a nursing instructor, contact
American Association of Colleges of Nursing
One Dupont Circle, NW, Suite 530
Washington, DC 20036-1135
Tel: 202-463-6930
http://www.aacn.nche.edu

For information on the nursing profession, contact
American Nurses Association
8515 Georgia Avenue, Suite 400
Silver Spring, MD 20910-3492
Tel: 800-274-4262
http://www.nursingworld.org

Discover Nursing, sponsored by Johnson & Johnson Services Inc., provides information on nursing careers, nursing schools, and scholarships.
Discover Nursing
http://www.discovernursing.com

Occupational Health Nurses

OVERVIEW

Occupational health nurses are registered nurses who care for people in the workplace. Although they treat illnesses, injuries, and health problems, they are also involved with safety and health issues and prevention programs. An occupational health nurse may be an employee of a business, institution, or corporation or may be self-employed on a contract or freelance basis. Some nurses may be a part of a team or company that provides occupational health services on a retainer or contract basis. There are approximately 30,000 occupational health nurses in the United States.

HISTORY

The first occupational health nurses— or industrial nurses as they were known at the time—were Ada Mayo Stewart and Betty Moulder. In 1885, Stewart was hired by the Vermont Marble Company to care for its employees and their families. Betty Moulder performed similar tasks for coal miners and their families in Pennsylvania in 1888. By the 1900s, industrial nurses were employed in U.S. factories to diagnose and limit the spread of infectious diseases and to help employers reduce costs arising from workers' compensation legislation. The field grew steadily during the first half of the 20th century, and in 1942, the American Association of Industrial Nurses (AAIN) was created to represent the professional interests of these specialized nurses. (In 1977, the AAIN changed its

QUICK FACTS

School Subjects
Biology
Chemistry

Personal Skills
Helping/teaching
Technical/scientific

Work Environment
Primarily indoors
One location with some
  travel

Minimum Education Level
Some postsecondary training

Salary Range
$43,970 to $63,750 to
  $95,142+

Certification or Licensing
Recommended (certification)
Required by all states
  (licensing)

Outlook
Much faster than the average

DOT
075

GOE
14.02.01

NOC
3152

O*NET-SOC
29-1111.00

name to the American Association of Occupational Health Nurses.) The Occupational Safety and Health Act of 1970 created a strong demand for occupational health nurses at work sites. According to the American Association of Occupational Health Nurses, today's occupational health nurses have expanded their duties beyond basic care to focus on case management, counseling and crisis intervention, health promotion, legal and regulatory compliance, and worker and workplace hazard detection.

THE JOB

Occupational health nurses provide health care services to the working population. These services may include emergency care in the case of an accident or critical illness, caring for ongoing work-related injuries such as back strain, or monitoring a worker's persistent high blood pressure or diabetes. Occupational health nurses are also responsible for assessing safety aspects of the workplace. Treating injuries includes analyzing how and why the injury occurred as well as initiating preventive measures in the plant or workplace.

On-site occupational health nurses may be required to treat illnesses and injuries and respond quickly to emergency situations or industrial accidents. They may also consult with an employee regarding medical insurance coverage, or an ongoing health problem such as high blood pressure, and they may serve as a one-on-one resource for general health and wellness information.

Cecelia Vaughn, RN, is a certified occupational health nurse specialist who works on a contract basis with a wide variety of clients. "When I go into a facility I have to look at all aspects of the work environment," she says. "Is the air clean? Is the worker exposed to harmful pollutants? Is the workplace lighting and ventilation satisfactory? Are workers tested periodically for chemical exposure, if necessary? Are safety programs presented on a regular basis?"

Vaughn adds, "I need to be able to relate personally to the workers. Are they stressed? Is the woman who has bruises a victim of abuse at home? Is a worker on drugs? Is there potential for violence at the workplace?"

Along with all the assessments and intervention, occupational health nurses are often responsible for making sure their company is following and documenting government-required workplace and health regulations. They may also be involved with company-sponsored health and safety workshops and may administer flu

Learn More About It

Katz, Janet R., Carol J. Carter, Joyce Bishop, and Sarah Lyman Kravits. *Keys to Nursing Success*. 3d ed. Upper Saddle River, N.J.: Prentice Hall, 2009.

Oakley, Katie, ed. *Occupational Health Nursing*. 3d ed. Hoboken, N.J.: Wiley, 2008.

Rogers, Bonnie, Susan A. Randolph, and Karen Mastroianni. *Occupational Health Nursing Guidelines for Primary Clinical Conditions*. 4th ed. Beverly Farms, Mass.: OEM Press Inc., 2009.

Salazar, Mary K., ed. *Core Curriculum for Occupational and Environmental Health Nursing*. 3d ed. St. Louis, Mo.: Saunders, 2005.

shots, be responsible for drug testing, and arrange for in-house mammograms and other wellness programs.

Like every nursing job, documentation and administration are important aspects of the duties. Occupational health nurses are usually responsible for reporting and documenting worker's compensation claims and for making sure the company meets Occupational Safety and Health Act requirements or other government workplace regulations.

Occupational health nurses ensure that workers who have special needs have safe, accommodating work stations. Teaching and demonstrating are also a big part of their responsibilities. Occupational health nurses may teach the proper way to lift heavy equipment to prevent back injury or train workers in cardiopulmonary resuscitation or emergency procedures.

"My job is so much fun," Vaughn says enthusiastically. "Every day is a new challenge. I never know what the day will bring, and my plans can change so quickly. If a company calls with an emergency situation, I might have to drop everything and go there."

REQUIREMENTS

High School

If you want to become an occupational health nurse, you will first need to become a registered nurse. (See the article "Registered Nurses.") To prepare for this career, you should take high school mathematics and science courses, including biology, chemistry, and physics. Health courses will also be helpful. English and speech courses should not be neglected because you must be able to communicate well with patients.

Postsecondary Training

It is preferred that nurses entering the occupational nursing field have a bachelor's degree in nursing (BSN) and nursing experience, especially in community health, ambulatory care, critical care, or emergency nursing.

Certification or Licensing

Licensing is mandatory to practice as a registered nurse. On the other hand, certification is voluntary and can be obtained through the American Board for Occupational Health Nurses. Certification reflects a mastery of the specialty practice in occupational health. Two levels of certification are available, depending on a candidate's level of education and experience: individuals can become a certified occupational health nurse or a certified occupational health nurse-specialist. See the end of this article for contact information.

Other Requirements

Because the duties of an occupational health nurse are so varied and unpredictable, the ability to think outside of the box is critical, according to Vaughn. "You must be able to look around a company and see the safety issues and the human issues, as well as the health issues. You must think about social responsibility. Is the work environment safe? Are harmful chemicals present? What emotional issues might employees be dealing with?" She adds, "This is a totally different kind of nursing than hospital bedside nursing."

Occupational health nurses should be able to think independently and make decisions quickly. They should have good management skills as well as the ability to relate well to all people in all positions.

EXPLORING

Volunteer at a local hospital to see what a nurse's day is like. Talk to as many medical professionals as possible in different fields to gauge your interest in all areas of the profession, including occupational health. Ask nurses what schools they attended and how hard the training was to complete. This should help you get an inside scoop on nursing programs.

Another good way to explore nursing is to visit hospitals that are sites for a nursing program's clinical rotations. You may even be able to attend an orientation for potential students.

EMPLOYERS

Approximately 30,000 occupational health nurses are employed in the United States. They are employed by corporations and companies of all sizes, by schools, and by government agencies.

STARTING OUT

The only way to become a registered nurse is through completion of one of the three kinds of educational programs plus passing the licensing examination. Registered nurses may apply for employment directly to hospitals, nursing homes, and companies and government agencies that hire nurses. Jobs can also be obtained through school career services offices, by signing up with employment agencies specializing in placement of nursing personnel, or through the state employment office. Other sources of jobs include professional journals and newspaper want ads. Additionally, the American Association of Occupational Health Nurses provides job listings at its Web site, https://www.aaohn.org.

ADVANCEMENT

Administrative and supervisory positions in the nursing field go to nurses who have earned at least the bachelor of science degree in nursing. Nurses with many years of experience who are graduates of the diploma program may achieve supervisory positions, but requirements for such promotions have become more difficult in recent years and in many cases require at least the bachelor of science in nursing degree.

EARNINGS

According to the U.S. Department of Labor (DOL), registered nurses earned a median salary of $63,750 in 2009. Salaries ranged from less than $43,970 to $93,700 or more a year.

However, occupational health nurses, because of their specialty, can generally expect to earn more. They typically earn salaries that range from $55,000 to $70,000 a year. *Occupational health nurse managers*, who are usually in charge of an organization's occupational health operations and manage a staff of nurses, made average annual salaries of $77,221 a year in November 2010, according to Salary.com. Salaries ranged from less than $63,147 to $95,142 or more a year.

Salary is determined by many factors, including nursing specialty, education, and place of employment, geographic location, and work experience. Flexible schedules and part-time employment opportunities are available for most nurses. Employers usually provide health and life insurance, and some offer educational reimbursements and year-end bonuses to their full-time staff.

WORK ENVIRONMENT

Occupational health nurses work in a variety of environments—from clean, healthy, well-lighted buildings to dusty, dirty, fume-filled manufacturing and mining facilities. Some nurses may have to spend time in hot manufacturing plants analyzing safety and environmental aspects of the workplace.

All nursing careers have some health and disease risks; however, adherence to health and safety guidelines greatly minimizes the chance of contracting infectious diseases such as hepatitis and AIDS. Medical knowledge and good safety measures are also needed to limit the nurse's exposure to toxic chemicals, radiation, and other hazards.

OUTLOOK

Nursing specialties will be in great demand in the future. The DOL predicts that employment for registered nurses is expected to increase much faster than the average for all careers through 2018.

More and more companies are realizing the value of healthy and happy employees who work in safe, environmentally conscious workplaces. While these views support the need for companies to hire occupational health nurses, the reality is that some companies see eliminating the in-house occupational health nurse as a way to save money. This downsizing then creates a need for outsourcing, which may increase the employment opportunities for independent occupational nurses or those employed with contract service companies.

The fact that we are becoming an older working America means new demands and new problems in the workforce. "We are now dealing with workers in their 60s and 70s," says Vaughn. "This fact alone creates additional justification for the services of the occupational health nurse."

FOR MORE INFORMATION

For information on nursing education and careers, contact
American Association of Colleges of Nursing
One Dupont Circle, NW, Suite 530
Washington, DC 20036-1135
Tel: 202-463-6930
http://www.aacn.nche.edu

For career and educational resources, contact
American Association of Occupational Health Nurses
7794 Grow Drive
Pensacola, FL 32514-7072
Tel: 800-241-8014
E-mail: aaohn@aaohn.org
https://www.aaohn.org

For information on certification, contact
American Board for Occupational Health Nurses
201 East Ogden Road, Suite 114
Hinsdale, IL 60521-3652
Tel: 888-842-2646
E-mail: info@abohn.org
http://www.abohn.org

For more general information on the field of occupational safety, visit the NIOSH Web site.
National Institute for Occupational Safety and Health (NIOSH)
Patriots Plaza Building
395 E Street, SW, Suite 9200
Washington, DC 20201-3298
Tel: 202-245-0625
http://www.cdc.gov/niosh

Oncological Nurses

QUICK FACTS

School Subjects
Biology
Chemistry

Personal Skills
Helping/teaching
Technical/scientific

Work Environment
Primarily indoors
Primarily one location

Minimum Education Level
Some postsecondary training

Salary Range
$43,970 to $63,750 to
$93,700+

Certification or Licensing
Recommended (certification)
Required by all states
(licensing)

Outlook
Much faster than the average

DOT
075

GOE
14.02.01

NOC
3152

O*NET-SOC
29-1111.00

OVERVIEW

Oncological nurses specialize in the treatment and care of cancer patients. While many oncological nurses care directly for cancer patients, some may be involved in patient or community education, cancer prevention, or cancer research. They may work in specific areas of cancer nursing, such as pediatrics, cancer rehabilitation, chemotherapy, biotherapy, hospice, pain management, and others.

HISTORY

The history of cancer dates back to early Greek and Roman writings, which included descriptions of the disease. Cancer affects all of the world's populations and has been the subject of intense medical investigations. According to the American Cancer Society, more than 1.5 million people in the United States are diagnosed with cancer each year. Cancer ranks second only to heart disease as the leading cause of death.

Nurses have always played a role in treating cancer patients, but it wasn't until the 1970s that oncological nurses began to receive greater recognition for their unique training and focus. The National Cancer Act of 1971 provided much-needed funding for cancer research, which improved the knowledge of oncological nurses. The First National Cancer Nursing Conference was held in 1973. A small group of oncological nurses met at this conference to discuss the possibility of creating a professional organization, and in 1975, The Oncology Nursing Society was created to represent the professional needs and interests of oncological nurses and other health care providers.

Developments in the late 20th century, such as improvements in cancer treatment and early detection, have advanced the discipline of oncology and led to further studies. In the 1950s, minor success with cytotoxic chemotherapy initiated active research to develop anticancer agents. Although most useful drugs have side effects, oncologists continue to conduct studies to find better treatments. Increased public awareness of the positive effects of a healthy diet and exercise as well as the harmful effects of smoking has helped lower the risk of developing many types of cancer. Many believe that cancer will someday become a largely preventable disease.

THE JOB

Carolyn Panhorst, a registered nurse, worked as an oncological nurse in a small hospital in a farming community in Indiana. "Our hospital was a satellite facility for a larger hospital in a metro area," states Panhorst. "Our doctors' offices were in the hospital, and I administered chemotherapy both to patients who were admitted to the hospital and to outpatients."

Because cancer treatment and care differ considerably depending on the facilities and the type of cancer the patient has, oncological nurses' job responsibilities vary greatly. It is important for them to keep up on current research, treatments, and other advances with the disease. Nurses who must administer drugs and other types of treatment must be aware of the changes in dosages, equipment, and side effects.

Panhorst relates, "Although technical expertise is definitely required when caring for cancer patients, the nurse needs to be emotionally and personally attached to the patient. If the nurse cannot give much of herself or himself, this is felt by the patient."

Caring for patients with cancer can be an emotional nursing experience. Nurses must be aware of the psychological aspects of this type of nursing. They also need to know the effects that this disease can have on the patients, families, and friends.

"'Don't get into this area and think you are going to save anybody,'" a nurse once told Panhorst. "I thought this was cold, but I understand now. You have to want to be there for your patients even though you may not be able to help them," says Panhorst. "You try to give them what science and technology knows, and then provide them with the best nursing care possible. But, you have to know that you are not God and leave your mind open to the full reality of what the possible outcome may be." She adds that you must be satisfied that you did the best you could.

"Taking care of cancer patients is a different kind of nursing," observes Panhorst. "In normal relationships people tend to be protective, but when patients are frightened by their illness, their pretense is gone. They have the ability to communicate more openly. They trust you with their innermost feelings, and that's a huge responsibility and also a privilege."

There are so many treatment choices available for cancer patients today that the nurse needs to be an educator as well as a caregiver. The nurse must help the patients receive the best possible care and also respect their wishes. "You need to be a patient advocate," says Panhorst. "You have to know the difference between giving them information and advising.

"This is an area of nursing where you can easily fall in love with your patient and their family," says Panhorst. "You can have a wonderful, meaningful relationship with the patient."

REQUIREMENTS

High School

If you want to become an oncological nurse, you will first need to become a registered nurse. (See the article "Registered Nurses.") To prepare for this career, you should take high school mathematics and science courses, including biology, chemistry, and physics. Health courses will also be helpful. English and speech courses should not be neglected because you must be able to communicate well with patients.

Postsecondary Training

You must be a registered nurse before you can become an oncological nurse. Entry-level requirements to become an oncological nurse depend on individual hiring qualifications of the institution or practice and the availability of nurses in that specialty and geographical region.

Certification or Licensing

Some institutions may require oncology nurses to be certified. The Oncology Nursing Certification Corporation offers the following certification designations: oncology certified nurse, certified pediatric hematology oncology nurse, certified breast care nurse, advanced oncology certified nurse practitioner, and advanced oncology certified clinical nurse specialist. Contact the corporation for more information (see For More Information at the end of this article).

All states and the District of Columbia require a license to practice nursing. To obtain a license, graduates of approved nursing schools must pass a national examination. Nurses may be licensed by more than one state. In some states, continuing education is a condition for license renewal.

Other Requirements

Oncological nurses should like working in a fast-paced environment that requires lifelong learning. New medical technology and treatment methods are constantly being developed and implemented. Oncological nurses should be technically inclined and be able to learn how to operate new medical equipment without feeling intimidated.

Because of the seriousness of their loved one's illness, family members and friends may be difficult to deal with and the nurse must display patience, understanding, compassion, and composure during these emotional times. The nurse must be able to communicate and explain medical terminology and procedures to the patient and family so they can make informed decisions and understand what is being done and why.

EXPLORING

You can explore your interest in the nursing field in a number of ways. You can read books about famous nurses (such as Clara Barton, Elizabeth Fry, or Florence Nightingale) or books on careers in nursing. You might also talk with your high school counselor, school nurse, or other nurses in your community about the career. You can also visit hospitals to observe the work of nurses.

Some hospitals now have extensive volunteer service programs in which students can work after school, on weekends, or during vacations. You can find other volunteer work experiences with the Red Cross or community health services. Camp counseling jobs sometimes offer related experiences. Some schools offer participation in Future Nurses programs.

To learn more about the specialty of oncology nursing, you should read books about cancer and the health care professionals who care for cancer patients, visit Web sites of associations such as The American Cancer Society (http://www.cancer.org), and talk with oncology nurses about their careers. Additionally, the Oncology Nursing Society offers a useful career guide at its Web site, http://www.onsconnect.org/careerguide. It also offers a Student Virtual Community at http://students.vc.ons.org.

EMPLOYERS

Oncological nurses practice in many professional settings, including AIDS, oncology, and medical surgical units, at hospitals, and cancer centers or treatment facilities. Some may be employed by private practice physicians, hospice programs, or by health education centers or research facilities. Some may work as public health nurses.

STARTING OUT

Oncology nurses must first become registered nurses by completing one of the three kinds of educational programs and passing the licensing examination. Registered nurses may apply for employment directly to hospitals, nursing homes, and companies and government agencies that hire nurses. Jobs can also be obtained through school career services offices, by signing up with employment agencies specializing in placement of nursing personnel, or through state employment offices. Other sources of jobs include professional journals, newspaper want ads, and Internet job and social networking sites. Additionally, the Oncology Nursing Society offers job listings at its Web site, http://www.ons.org.

ADVANCEMENT

Administrative and supervisory positions in the nursing field go to nurses who have earned at least the bachelor of science degree in nursing. Nurses with many years of experience who are graduates of the diploma program may achieve supervisory positions, but requirements for such promotions have become more difficult in recent years and in many cases require at least the bachelor of science in nursing degree.

EARNINGS

Salary is determined by many factors, including nursing specialty, education, and place of employment, shift worked, geographical location, and work experience.

According to the U.S. Department of Labor, registered nurses earned a median salary of $63,750 in 2009. The lowest paid 10 percent earned less than $43,970, while the middle 50 percent earned between $52,520 and $77,970. The top paid 10 percent made $93,700 or more a year. However, many oncological nurses, because of their specialized skills, earn more.

Flexible schedules and part-time employment opportunities are available for most nurses. Employers usually provide health and life insurance, and some offer educational reimbursements and year-end bonuses to their full-time staff.

WORK ENVIRONMENT

Some oncological nurses may work in clean, well-lighted hospitals, clinics, and other health care settings in upscale communities, while others may find themselves working in remote, underdeveloped areas that have poor conditions. Personal safety may be an issue at times.

Generally, oncological nurses who wish to advance in their careers will find themselves working in larger hospitals or medical centers in major cities.

All nursing careers have some health and disease risks; however, adherence to health and safety guidelines greatly minimizes the chance of contracting infectious diseases such as hepatitis and AIDS. Medical knowledge and good safety measures are also needed to limit the nurse's exposure to toxic chemicals, radiation, and other hazards.

Long hours and intense nursing demands can create "burn-out" for some nurses, meaning that they often become dissatisfied with their jobs. Fortunately, there are many areas in which nurses can use their skills, so sometimes trying a different type of nursing may be the answer.

OUTLOOK

Nursing specialties will be in great demand in the future. The U.S. Bureau of Labor Statistics projects that between 2008 and 2018 employment for registered nurses will grow much faster than the average for all occupations.

The outlook for oncological nurses is excellent. The U.S. Bureau of the Census estimates that the number of individuals aged 65 or older will double by 2050. As our population grows older, the need for oncological nursing will increase because older people are more likely to be diagnosed with cancer. In addition, managed care organizations will continue to need nurses to provide health promotion and disease prevention programs to their subscribers.

Job opportunities vary across the country and may be available in all geographic areas. Home health care will be a growing nursing area. (See "Home Health Care and Hospice Nurses.") More services will be delivered in a home setting, and patients will receive transfusions, chemotherapy treatments, and medications through home health visits.

FOR MORE INFORMATION

For information on nursing education and careers, contact
American Association of Colleges of Nursing
One Dupont Circle, NW, Suite 530
Washington, DC 20036-1135
Tel: 202-463-6930
http://www.aacn.nche.edu

For information on various levels of certification, contact
Oncology Nursing Certification Corporation
125 Enterprise Drive
Pittsburgh, PA 15275-1214
Tel: 877-769-6622
E-mail: oncc@ons.org
http://www.oncc.org

For information on the oncological specialty, contact
Oncology Nursing Society
125 Enterprise Drive
Pittsburgh, PA 15275-1214
Tel: 866-257-4667
http://www.ons.org

INTERVIEW

Carol S. Blecher, RN, MS, AOCN, APNC, is an advanced practice oncological nurse at Trinitas Comprehensive Cancer Center in Elizabeth, New Jersey. She discussed her career with the editors of Careers in Focus: Nursing.

Q. How long have you worked in the field? What made you want to enter this career?

A. I have been an oncological nurse since 1983. I became certified in 1988 and earned my master's degree in 1989. I became an oncological nurse because I discovered that I could learn much about living and identifying the things that are important in life from patients with an oncology diagnosis. I have also learned about courage and dignity in face of a major life stressor.

Q. What is one thing that young people may not know about a career in oncological nursing?

A. The most important thing to remember is that a career in oncological nursing is not depressing. People always ask me why I chose a profession that "is so depressing." My reply is that oncological nursing is definitely not depressing. We learn from our patients how to celebrate victories, however small, and to live and enjoy each day to the fullest. Celebrating life is always important and when you work with patients with a chronic disease, such as cancer, you celebrate all of life's occasions, large and small.

Q. What are the most important personal and professional qualities for oncological nurses?

A. The most important personal qualities for oncological nurses are empathy and caring. This is a very difficult time for both the patients and their caregivers. All of these individuals need to feel that they are cared for as well as cared about. It is vital that the oncological nurse be knowledgeable and achieve certification in oncology, so that he or she can provide quality nursing care and administer treatments in a safe manner. They also need to be educators, teaching the patients and their caregivers about the disease, side effects of the treatments, and how to care for themselves during and after treatment.

Q. What are some of the pros and cons of your job?

A. The pros are the satisfaction that can be derived from caring for patients and their caregivers. When novice nurses are growing within the field, learning about oncological nursing, and achieving certification within the profession, there is a true sense of accomplishment for them and for their mentors. Mentoring nurses and helping them find their niche in oncology nursing, be it in community outreach, clinical trials, patient navigation, staff education, palliative care, or hospice, has always been a rewarding part of my job. The fact that people are living longer and better lives with a diagnosis of cancer is a major accomplishment and nurses play a very important role in supporting patients and families in living with cancer.

The negative aspect of my job is that the work both with staff and patients can be draining, and I always have to remember to be kind to myself in order to prevent burnout. I think that this is important for all nurses, because if we burn out and cannot share with others we lose our effectiveness. Another difficult part of my job is dealing with the death of a person to whom

I have become attached, but if I have been able to assure that the person and their caregivers have quality time together it makes it easier to deal with death.

Q. What advice would you give to young people who are interested in the field?

A. I would suggest that young people do volunteer work in any field that interests them to try to determine if they enjoy the area. There is a great need for volunteers in the workforce and in doing this type of work a person can learn about the field and assess their comfort level within the area while performing a great service to the community. You also must love the sciences in order to enter any of the health care professions. Communication skills are vital, as you are always communicating on many levels with fellow staff members, doctors, patients, caregivers, and other members of the health care team. A love of people is imperative for anyone interested in oncology nursing. My advice is always to follow your dreams and make what might seem impossible happen. It is not an easy road to travel, but the rewards are well worth the journey.

Q. What is the employment outlook for oncological nurses? How is the field changing?

A. I think that the employment outlook for nursing in general and oncological nursing, in particular, is excellent. Within the next 10 to 15 years many nurses will be retiring, as the average age of the nurses today is between the ages of 44 and 47. This will create a need for large numbers of new oncological nurses to replace the ones leaving the workforce. There are many predictions that future entry-level nurses will need a bachelor's degree, appropriately raising the standard of care. We will need more advanced practitioners and physician extenders, as there are also predictions that there will be a shortage of physicians. Nurses will be required to practice at higher levels of competency and provide more of the direct patient care in the areas of clinical trials, survivorship care, as well as assisting patients and caregivers in navigating the health care system. Obviously we will also need nurse educators to educate new nurses and to provide continuing education and challenges for experienced staff. We will also need nurse researchers to continue the evidence-based practice initiatives. I believe that the opportunities in oncological nursing are as varied as the disease itself and as we learn more, the prospects become greater.

Physician Assistants

OVERVIEW

Physician assistants (PAs) practice medicine under the supervision of licensed doctors of medicine or osteopathy, providing various health care services to patients. Much of the work they do was formerly limited to physicians. Although PAs are not nurses, they share responsibilities with registered nurses and nurse practitioners. Many PAs begin their careers in another health care occupation such as registered nurse or emergency medical technician. There are approximately 74,800 PAs employed in the United States.

HISTORY

PAs are fairly recent additions to the health care profession. The occupation originated in the 1960s when many medical corpsmen received additional education enabling them to help physicians with various medical tasks. In 1967, Duke University's physician assistant program graduated the first class of students who were formally known as physician assistants. Since then, the work of the PA has grown and expanded; in addition, the number of PAs in the United States has greatly increased. Fewer than 100 PAs were practicing in 1970; today there are approximately 74,800.

THE JOB

PAs help physicians provide medical care to patients. PAs may be assigned a variety of tasks; they may take medical histories of patients, do complete routine physical examinations, order labora-

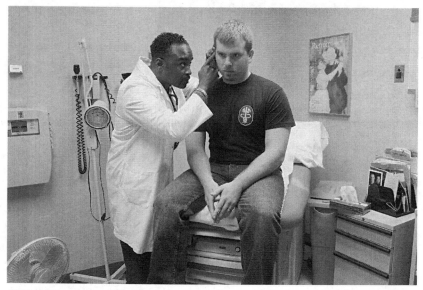

A physician assistant examines a patient. *(Matt Nelson,* The Gazette/
AP Photo)

tory tests, draw blood samples, give injections, decide on diagno-
ses, choose treatments, and assist in surgery. Although the duties
of PAs vary by state, they always work under the supervision and
direction of a licensed physician. The extent of the PA's duties
depends on the specific laws of the state and the practices of the
supervising physician, as well as the experience and abilities of
the PA. PAs work in a variety of health care settings, including
hospitals, clinics, physician's offices, and federal, state, and local
agencies.

More than 35 percent of all PAs specialize in general medicine,
such as family medicine, internal medicine, general pediatrics, and
obstetrics and gynecology, according to the 2009 AAPA Physician
Assistant Census. More than 25 percent are in general surgery/
surgical subspecialties, 10.3 percent specialize in emergency medicine, and 10.8 percent are in internal medicine subspecialties.

All 50 states, the District of Columbia, and Guam allow PAs to
prescribe medicine to patients.

PAs are skilled professionals who assume a great deal of responsibility in their work. By handling various medical tasks for their
physician employers, PAs allow physicians more time to diagnose
and treat more severely ill patients.

REQUIREMENTS

High School

Since a PA needs to be good with numbers and understand how the human body works, anyone interested in this job can begin preparing in high school by taking math classes and science classes, such as biology and chemistry, as well as health classes. English and social science classes, such as psychology, will also help you improve your communication skills and give you an understanding of people.

Also, keep in mind that it's not too early to gain some experience in the health care field. Many postsecondary institutions take into consideration an applicant's hands-on experience when deciding whom to accept, so look for paid or volunteer positions in your community.

Postsecondary Training

Most states require that PAs complete an educational program approved by the Accreditation Review Commission on Education for the Physician Assistant (http://www.arc-pa.org). There are approximately 142 fully or provisionally accredited PA programs. Admissions requirements vary, but two years of college courses in science or health, and some health care experience, are usually the minimum requirements. The American Academy of Physician Assistants (AAPA) reports that a majority of all students accepted, however, have their bachelor's or master's degrees. Most educational programs last 24 to 32 months, although some last only one year and others may last as many as three years.

The first six to 24 months of most programs involve classroom instruction in human anatomy, biochemistry, pathology, physiology, microbiology, clinical pharmacology, applied psychology, clinical medicine, and medical ethics. During the last months of most programs, students engage in supervised clinical work, usually including assignments, or rotations, in various branches of medicine, such as family practice, pediatrics, and emergency medicine.

Graduates of these programs may receive a certificate, an associate's degree, a bachelor's degree, or a master's degree; most programs, however, offer graduates a bachelor's degree. The one MEDEX program that presently exists (at the University of Washington, http://www.washington.edu/medicine/som/depts/medex) lasts only 18 months. It is designed for medical corpsmen, registered nurses, and others who have had extensive patient-care experience. MEDEX students usually obtain most of their clinical experience by working with a physician who will hire them after graduation.

PA programs are offered in a variety of educational and health care settings, including colleges and universities, medical schools and centers, hospitals, and the armed forces. State laws and regulations dictate the scope of the PA's duties, and, in all but a few states, PAs must be graduates of an approved training program.

Certification or Licensing

Currently, all states require that PAs be certified by the National Commission on Certification of Physician Assistants (NCCPA). To become certified, applicants must be graduates of an accredited PA program and pass the Physician Assistant National Certifying Examination (PANCE). After successfully completing the examination, PAs can use the credential, physician assistant-certified.

Once certified, PAs are required to complete 100 hours of continuing medical education courses every two years, and in addition must pass a recertification examination every six years. Besides NCCPA certification, most states also require that PAs register with the state medical board. State rules and regulations vary greatly concerning the work of PAs, and applicants are advised to study the laws of the state in which they wish to practice.

Licensing for PAs varies by state. New graduates should contact their state's licensing board to find out about specific requirements. Some states grant temporary licenses to PAs who have applied for the PANCE. For permanent licensure, most states require verification of certification or an official record of their exam scores.

Other Requirements

To be a successful PA, you must be able to work well with many different kinds of people, from the physician who supervises you to the many different patients you see every day. In addition to being a caring individual, you should also have a strong desire to continue learning in order to keep up with the latest medical procedures and recertification requirements. Since ill individuals depend on a PA's decisions, anyone interested in this job should have leadership skills and self-confidence as well as compassion.

EXPLORING

If you are interested in exploring the profession, talk with school counselors, practicing PAs, PA students, and various health care employees at local hospitals and clinics. You can also obtain information by contacting one of the organizations listed at the end of this article. Working as a volunteer in a hospital, clinic, or nursing home is a good way to get exposure to the health care profession. In addition, while in college, you may be able to obtain summer jobs as a hospital orderly, nurse assistant, or medical clerk. Such jobs can help you assess your interest in and suitability for work as a PA before you apply to a PA program.

EMPLOYERS

Approximately 74,800 PAs are employed in the United States. PAs work in a variety of health care settings. According to the AAPA, 44 percent of all PAs are employed by single physicians or group practices; 37.5 percent are employed by hospitals. They are also employed by clinics, nursing homes, long-term care facilities, and prisons. Many areas lacking quality medical care personnel, such as remote rural areas and the inner city, are hiring PAs to meet their needs.

STARTING OUT

PAs must complete their formal training programs before entering the job market. Once they complete their studies, PA students can utilize the career services offices of their schools to locate jobs. PAs may also seek employment at hospitals, clinics, medical offices, or other health care settings. Information about jobs with the federal government can be obtained by contacting the Office of Personnel Management's Web site at http://www.usajobs.opm.gov.

ADVANCEMENT

There are several ways for PAs to advance. Hospitals, for example, do not employ head PAs. Those with experience can assume more responsibility at higher pay, or they move on to employment at larger hospitals and clinics. Some PAs go back to school for additional education to practice in a specialty area, such as surgery, urology, or ophthalmology.

EARNINGS

Salaries of PAs vary according to experience, specialty, and employer. The median annual average for all PAs was $93,496 in 2009, according to the 2009 AAPA Physician Assistant Census. The U.S. Department of Labor (DOL) reports that the lowest paid 10 percent of all PAs earned less than $55,880 in 2009, and the highest paid 10 percent earned $115,080 or more. It also reports that PAs employed in offices and clinics of medical doctors had mean annual earnings of $84,720, while those employed in hospitals earned $86,850. PAs are well compensated compared with other occupations that have similar training requirements. Most PAs receive health and life insurance among other benefits.

WORK ENVIRONMENT

Most work settings are comfortable and clean, although, like physicians, PAs spend a good part of their day standing or walking. The workweek varies according to the employment setting. A few emergency room PAs may work 24-hour shifts, twice a week; others work 12-hour shifts, three times a week. PAs who work in physicians' offices, hospitals, or clinics may have to work weekends, nights, and holidays. PAs employed in clinics, however, usually work five-day, 40-hour weeks.

OUTLOOK

Employment for physician assistants, according to the DOL, is expected to increase much faster than the average for all occupations through 2018 because the health care industry is continuing to use more PAs to reduce costs. Opportunities will be best in rural areas and inner city clinics—settings that often have trouble attracting the most qualified candidates.

The role of the PA in delivering health care has also expanded over the past decade. PAs have taken on new duties and responsibilities, and they now work in a variety of health care settings. The DOL reports that physician assistants should have good opportunities in hospitals, academic medical centers, public clinics, prisons, and inpatient teaching hospitals.

FOR MORE INFORMATION

For more information on PA careers, educational programs, and scholarships, contact
  American Academy of Physician Assistants
  950 North Washington Street
  Alexandria, VA 22314-1552
  Tel: 703-836-2272

E-mail: aapa@aapa.org
http://www.aapa.org

For information on certification, contact
National Commission on Certification of Physician Assistants
12000 Findley Road, Suite 100
Duluth, GA 30097-1484
Tel: 678-417-8100
E-mail: nccpa@nccpa.net
http://www.nccpa.net

For industry information and to subscribe ($35 fee) to the PA Programs Directory, *contact*
Physician Assistant Education Association
300 North Washington Street, Suite 710
Alexandria, VA 22314-2544
Tel: 703-548-5538
E-mail: info@paeaonline.org
http://www.paeaonline.org

This Web site offers information on issues affecting PAs and provides links to other sites of interest.
Advance for Nurse Practitioners and Physician Assistants
http://nurse-practitioners-and-physician-assistants.advanceweb
.com/Default.aspx

Psychiatric Nurses

QUICK FACTS

School Subjects
Biology
Chemistry

Personal Skills
Helping/teaching
Technical/scientific

Work Environment
Primarily indoors
Primarily one location

Minimum Education Level
Some postsecondary training

Salary Range
$35,000 to $60,000 to
$100,140+

Certification or Licensing
Voluntary (certification)
Required by all states
(licensing)

Outlook
Much faster than the average

DOT
075

GOE
14.02.01

NOC
3151, 3152

O*NET-SOC
29-1111.00

OVERVIEW

Psychiatric nurses focus on mental health. This includes the prevention of mental illness and the maintenance of good mental health, as well as the diagnosis and treatment of mental disorders. They care for pediatric, teen, adult, and elderly patients who may have a broad spectrum of mentally and emotionally related medical needs. In addition to providing individualized nursing care, psychiatric nurses serve as consultants, conduct research, and work in management and administrative positions in institutions and corporations. The American Psychiatric Nurses Association (APNA) has more than 6,500 members.

HISTORY

Although some mentally ill people were treated as early as the 15th century in institutions like the Hospital of Saint Mary of Bethlehem in London, the practice of institutionalizing people with mental disorders did not become common until the 17th century.

During the 17th, 18th, and even into the 19th centuries, treatment of mentally ill patients was quite crude and often simply barbarous. This state of affairs started to change as medical practitioners began to see mental illness as a medical problem. During the late 18th and early 19th centuries, hospitals began concentrating on keeping patients clean and comfortable, building their self-respect, and treating them with friendliness and encouragement. This method of treating mental illness resulted in the establishment of specially designed institutions for the care of mental patients.

Linda Richards is considered to be the first psychiatric nurse in the United States. In 1882, she opened the Boston City Hospital Training School for Nurses to educate nurses in the care of psychiatric patients. But it wasn't until more than 30 years later that the first psychiatric nursing program of study within the curriculum of a nursing school was established. Such training was gradually added to nursing school programs throughout the United States and Canada.

The National Mental Health Act of 1946 created a strong interest in mental health issues and the educational preparation for psychiatric nurses and other professionals in the field. In 1954, the first graduate program in psychiatric nursing was started at Rutgers University.

The American Psychiatric Nurses Association has emerged as the leading voice of psychiatric nurses in the United States. It has more than 6,400 members involved in inpatient and outpatient levels of care.

THE JOB

According to the APNA, psychiatric nursing occurs at two levels—*psychiatric-mental health nurse* (PMHN) and advanced. Psychiatric-mental health nurses are registered nurses who work primarily with patients needing mental health or psychiatric care.

Advanced practice psychiatric nurses are also registered nurses but they have earned certification as certified nurse specialists or have taken graduate courses to become clinical nurse specialists or nurse practitioners, or psychiatric nurse practitioners. Some of these specialists may work in supervisory or administrative positions and may, depending on their state's laws, be able to provide psychotherapy services and prescribe medications. Psychiatric nurses in this second, more advanced group may sub-specialize in areas such as child-adolescent mental health nursing, geropsychiatric nursing, forensic nursing, or substance abuse nursing.

Psychiatric nurses perform a wide range of direct-care nursing duties for the mentally ill, emotionally disturbed, and developmentally handicapped. They may work with individuals, groups, families, and communities. They care for all people, including children, teens, adults, and the elderly.

In addition to direct patient care, some psychiatric nurses may use their training in the community as community health nurses (See "Community Health Nurses") or educators (See "Nursing Instructors"). They may also work for insurance or managed care companies, or in health care institutions or government facilities in an administrative, supervisory, or research position. Other nurses may be self-employed on a consulting or contract basis.

Psychiatric nursing is a very intense nursing specialty. Patients require constant attention, mental and physical care, and monitoring.

REQUIREMENTS

High School

Psychiatric nurses must first be registered nurses. (See the article "Registered Nurses.") To prepare for this career, you should take high school mathematics and science courses, including biology, chemistry, and physics. Health courses will also be helpful. English and speech courses should not be neglected because you must be able to communicate well with patients.

Postsecondary Training

Entry-level requirements to become a psychiatric nurse depend on the state, the institution, its size, who it serves, and the availability of nurses in that specialty and geographical region. Usually nurses must have some nursing experience before entering the psychiatric nursing field. Some institutions may require certification as a psychiatric nurse. Psychiatric nurses who wish to advance their education may take graduate level courses and become certified nurse specialists or nurse practitioners.

Certification or Licensing

Psychiatric nurses who are registered nurses who meet experience and education requirements can become certified by the American Nurses Credentialing Center.

All states and the District of Columbia require a license to practice nursing. To obtain a license, graduates of approved nursing schools must pass a national examination. Nurses may be licensed by more than one state. In some states, continuing education is a condition for license renewal. Different titles require different education and training levels.

Other Requirements

Psychiatric nurses should like working in a fast-paced environment that requires lifelong learning. Research into human behavior and the brain is constantly resulting in new information regarding patient care, drug therapy, and treatments.

In many cases, psychiatric nurses are confronted with situations that may require them to act immediately, independently, and confidently, so they must have good decision-making skills. They must also be good team players and able to get along with people from all walks of life. They must work with patients and families as well as other medical, administrative, and institutional personnel.

Psychiatric nurses must be able to deal with people in a troubling time of their lives. They must be able to communicate with the families and friends of persons with mental problems who may find the illness difficult to understand. Nurses need to display patience, understanding, and composure during these emotional times.

Many facilities require nurses to work 10- to 12-hour shifts, which can be very exhausting. In addition, nurses are often on call.

EXPLORING

To explore the field of nursing further, read up on the field as much as possible. The Internet and your local library are great resources for additional information. Talk to your school's career counselor about your possible interest in health care. He or she may be able to suggest different nursing programs to research or, better yet, give you names of previous students to talk to who have gone on to these medical programs. Volunteering at local hospitals or health care clinics can give you experience working with patients.

Specific to psychiatric nursing, do some research on topics such as drug and alcohol dependence, depression, and other concerns of the field to learn more about this specialized area of nursing.

EMPLOYERS

The APNA has more than 6,500 members. Psychiatric nurses are employed in hospitals, psychiatric and mental health facilities, in doctors' offices, in correctional institutions, in nursing homes, in shelters, and in group homes.

STARTING OUT

Psychiatric nurses must usually work as registered nurses before they can specialize in psychiatric nursing. To become a registered nurse, they must complete one of the three kinds of educational programs and pass the licensing examination. Registered nurses may apply for employment directly to hospitals, nursing homes, and companies and government agencies that hire nurses. Jobs can also be obtained through school career services offices, by signing up with employment agencies specializing in placement of nursing personnel, or through the state employment office. Other sources of jobs include professional journals, newspaper want ads, and employment Web sites. Additionally, the APNA offers job listings at its Web site, http://www.apna.org.

ADVANCEMENT

Administrative and supervisory positions in the nursing field go to nurses who have earned at least the bachelor of science degree in nursing (BSN). Nurses with many years of experience who are graduates of the diploma program may achieve supervisory positions, but requirements for such promotions have become more difficult in recent years and in many cases require at least the bachelor of science in nursing degree.

EARNINGS

According to the APNA, psychiatric–mental health nurses earn starting salaries that range from $35,000 to $40,000 annually. Advanced practice psychiatric nurses earn salaries that range from $60,000 to more than $80,000 a year. In a 2009 salary survey conducted by *ADVANCE for Nurse Practitioners*, the average annual salary for nurse practitioners in mental health care was $100,140. According to the U.S. Department of Labor (DOL), registered nurses made a median annual salary of $63,750 in 2009, with salaries ranging from less than $43,970 to more than $93,700 a year.

Salary is determined by many factors, including nursing specialty, education, place of employment, shift worked, geographical location, and work experience. Flexible schedules and part-time employment opportunities are available for most nurses. Employers usually provide health and life insurance, and some offer educational reimbursements and year-end bonuses to their full-time staff.

WORK ENVIRONMENT

Government institutions, corporations, businesses, nursing homes, correctional institutions, research facilities, and hospitals may employ psychiatric nurses. Most hospital and institutional environments are clean and well lighted. Inner city facilities and hospitals may be in less than desirable locations and safety may be an issue.

Generally, psychiatric nurses who wish to advance in their careers will find themselves working in larger facilities in major cities.

All nursing careers have some health and disease risks; however, adherence to health and safety guidelines greatly minimizes the chance of contracting infectious diseases such as hepatitis and AIDS. Medical knowledge and good safety measures are also needed to limit the nurse's exposure to toxic chemicals, radiation, and other hazards. In addition, psychiatric nurses may be exposed to violent and unpredictable behavior, which may increase their risk of injury.

Nurses usually spend much of the day on their feet, either walking or standing. Many hospital nurses work 10- or 12-hour shifts, which can be tiring. Long hours and intense nursing demands can create burnout for some nurses, meaning that they often become dissatisfied with their jobs. Fortunately, there are many areas in which nurses can use their skills, so sometimes trying a different type of nursing may be the answer.

OUTLOOK

Mental illness is a leading cause of disability in the United States and mental disorders affect one in five Americans, including children, adolescents, adults, and the elderly. The need for psychiatric and other nursing specialties will be in great demand in the future. The DOL projects that employment for registered nurses will grow much faster than the average for all occupations through 2018.

FOR MORE INFORMATION

For information on educational programs, contact
American Association of Colleges of Nursing
One Dupont Circle, NW, Suite 530
Washington, DC 20036-1135
Tel: 202-463-6930
http://www.aacn.nche.edu

For information on certification, contact
American Nurses Credentialing Center
8515 Georgia Avenue, Suite 400
Silver Spring, MD 20910-3492
Tel: 800-284-2378
http://www.nursecredentialing.org

For information on education, careers, and certification, contact
American Psychiatric Nurses Association
1555 Wilson Boulevard, Suite 530
Arlington, VA 22209-2405
Tel: 866-243-2443
http://www.apna.org

Registered Nurses

OVERVIEW

Registered nurses (RNs) help individuals, families, and groups to achieve health and prevent disease. They care for the sick and injured in hospitals and other health care facilities, physicians' offices, private homes, public health agencies, schools, camps, and industry. Some RNs are employed in private practice. RNs hold about 2.6 million jobs in the United States.

HISTORY

Modern ideas about hospitals and nursing as a profession did not develop until the 19th century. The life and work of Florence Nightingale were a strong influence on the profession's development. Nightingale, who came from a wealthy, upper-class British family, dedicated her life to improving conditions in hospitals, beginning in an army hospital during the Crimean War. In the United States, many of Nightingale's ideas were put into practice for the care of the wounded during the Civil War. The care, however, was provided by concerned individuals who nursed rather than by trained nurses. They had not received the kind of training that is required for nurses today.

The first school of nursing in the United States was founded in Boston in 1873. In 1938, New York State passed the first state law to require that practical nurses be licensed. The establishment of other schools followed, but the training programs lacked uniformity.

After the 1938 law was passed, a movement began to have organized training programs that would assure new standards in the field. The role and training of nurses have undergone radical changes since the first schools were opened.

Education standards for nurses have been improving constantly since that time. Today's nurse is a highly educated, licensed health care professional. Extended programs of training are offered throughout the country, and all states have enacted laws to assure training standards are maintained and to assure qualification for licensure. Nurses are a vital part of the health care system.

THE JOB

RNs work under the direct supervision of nursing departments and in collaboration with physicians. Sixty percent of all registered nurses work in hospitals, where they may be assigned to general, operating room, or maternity room duty. They may also care for sick children or be assigned to other hospital units, such as emergency rooms, intensive care units, or outpatient clinics. There are many different kinds of RNs. The following paragraphs detail some of the many opportunities in registered nursing. (Read the separate articles for many of these nursing specialties.)

General duty nurses work together with other members of the health care team to assess the patient's condition and to develop and implement a plan of health care. These nurses may perform such tasks as taking patients' vital signs, administering medication and injections, recording the symptoms and progress of patients, changing dressings, assisting patients with personal care, conferring with members of the medical staff, helping prepare a patient for surgery, and completing any number of duties that require skill and understanding of patients' needs.

Surgical nurses oversee the preparation of the operating room and the sterilization of instruments. They assist surgeons during operations and coordinate the flow of patient cases in operating rooms. Surgical nurses include *floor nurses* (who work on surgical units) and *perioperative nurses*. There are several kinds of perioperative nurses. *Day surgery pre-op nurses* check patients in and get them ready for the day's surgery. *Scrub nurses* select and organize supplies and medical instruments that will be used during the surgery. The *circulating nurse* is a non-sterile member of the surgical team. Scrub and circulating nurses are also called *intra-op nurses*. *Post anesthesia care unit nurses* take over from the intra-op nurses once the surgery is completed. They assess the patient for pain, breathing, bleeding, general vital signs, etc. They are also known as *post-op nurses* and *recovery room nurses*. Additionally, *RN first assistants* are a relatively new type of surgical nurse who work directly with surgeons in the operating room and in office settings seeing pre- and post-op patients. They may also check on pre- and post-op patients, but they are not floor nurses. *Critical care nurses* provide highly skilled direct patient care to critically ill patients needing intense medical treatment. Contrary to previously held beliefs that critical care nurses work only in intensive care units or cardiac care units of hospitals, today's critical care nurses work in the emergency departments, post anesthesia recovery units, pediatric intensive care units, burn units, and neonatal intensive care units of medical facilities, as well as in other units that treat critically ill patients.

Maternity nurses, or *neonatal nurses*, help in the delivery room, take care of newborns in the nursery, and teach mothers how to feed and care for their babies.

The activities of *staff nurses* are directed and coordinated by *head nurses* and *charge nurses*. Heading up the entire nursing program in the hospital is the *nursing service director*, who administers the nursing program to maintain standards of patient care. The *nursing service director* advises the medical staff, department heads, and the hospital administrator in matters relating to nursing services and helps prepare the department budget.

Private duty nurses may work in hospitals or in a patient's home. They are employed by the patient they are caring for or by the patient's family. Their service is designed for the individual care of one person and is carried out in cooperation with the patient's physician.

Office nurses usually work in the office of a dentist, physician, or health maintenance organization (HMO). An office nurse may be one of several nurses on the staff or the only staff nurse. If a nurse is the only staff member, this person may have to combine some clerical duties with those of nursing, such as serving as receptionist, making appointments for the doctor, helping maintain patient records, sending out monthly statements, and attending to routine correspondence. If the physician's staff is a large one that includes secretaries and clerks, the office nurse will concentrate on screening patients, assisting with examinations, supervising the examining rooms, sterilizing equipment, providing patient education, and performing other nursing duties.

Occupational health nurses, or *industrial nurses*, are an important part of many large firms. They maintain a clinic at a plant or factory and are usually occupied in rendering preventive, remedial, and educational nursing services. They work under the direction of an industrial physician, nursing director, or nursing supervisor. They may advise on accident prevention, visit employees on the job to check the conditions under which they work, and advise management about the safety of such conditions. At the plant, they render treatment in emergencies.

School nurses may work in one school or in several, visiting each for a part of the day or week. They may supervise the student clinic, treat minor cuts or injuries, or give advice on good health practices. They may examine students to detect conditions of the eyes or teeth that require attention. They also assist the school physician.

Community health nurses, also called *public health nurses*, require specialized training for their duties. Their job usually requires them to spend part of the time traveling from one assignment to another. Their duties may differ greatly from one case to another. For instance, in one day they may have to instruct a class of expectant mothers, visit new parents to help them plan proper care for the baby, visit an aged patient requiring special care, and conduct a class in nutrition. They usually possess many and varied nursing skills and often are called upon to meet unexpected or unusual situations.

Dermatology nurses treat patients with diseases and ailments of the skin, hair, mucous membranes, nails, and related tissues or structures.

Oncological nurses specialize in the treatment and care of cancer patients. While many oncological nurses care directly for cancer patients, some may be involved in patient or community education, cancer prevention, or cancer research. They may work in specific areas of cancer nursing, such as pediatrics, cancer rehabilitation, chemotherapy, biotherapy, hospice, pain management, and others.

Forensic nurses examine victims of crimes such as sexual assault, domestic abuse, child abuse, or elder abuse. They gather evidence and information for law enforcement officials. They may also gather evidence at crime scenes or in other settings.

Nurse informaticists organize and manage nursing data to help patients, nurses, managers, policy makers, and other health care professionals make better decisions.

Home health care nurses, also called *visiting nurses*, provide home-based health care under the direction of a physician. They care for persons who may be recovering from an accident, illness, surgery, cancer, or childbirth. They may work for a community organization, a private health care provider, or they may be independent nurses who work on a contract basis.

While home health care nurses care for patients expecting to recover, *hospice nurses* care for people who are in the final stages of a terminal illness. Typically, a hospice patient has less than six months to live. Hospice nurses provide medical and emotional support to the patients and their families and friends. Hospice care usually takes place in the patient's home, but patients may also receive hospice care in a hospital room, nursing home, or a relative's home.

Administrators in the community health field include *nursing directors, educational directors*, and *nursing supervisors*. Some nurses go into nursing education and work with nursing students to instruct them on theories and skills they will need to enter the profession. *Nursing instructors* may give classroom instruction and demonstrations or supervise nursing students on hospital units. Some instructors eventually become nursing school directors, university faculty, or deans of a university degree program. Nurses also have the opportunity to direct staff development and continuing education programs for nursing personnel in hospitals.

Advanced practice nurses are nurses with training beyond that required to have the RN designation. There are four primary categories of nurses included in this category: *nurse-midwives, clinical nurse specialists, nurse anesthetists*, and *nurse practitioners*. (See the separate articles on each of these careers.)

Nursing Informatics

Because of the increasingly complex nature of today's health care environment, now more than ever before nurses can fuse their less traditional nursing skills with their medical careers. *Nursing informatics* is just one area that enables nurses to do this. Nursing informatics is a broad field that enables nurses with interests in computer, information, and communication systems to improve daily work in nursing units, thereby creating better patient care. Jobs in nursing informatics are varied. For example, an *informatics nurse* can be a *nurse programmer* who builds the applications that other nurses will use, or a *clinical nurse* who is responsible for assessing and implementing communication systems in nursing units. Informatics nurses can also work for technology manufacturers in, for example, research and development of new nursing products or as *field consultants* who train other nurses in how to use new technologies.

Visit the following Web sites for more information on nursing informatics: Healthcare Information and Management Systems Society: Nursing Informatics (http://www.himss.org/ASP/topics_nursingInformatics.asp) and Nursing-Informatics.com (http://www.nursing-informatics.com). For a list of nursing informatics programs, visit http://www.allnursingschools.com/featured/nursing-informatics.php.

Some nurses are consultants to hospitals, nursing schools, industrial organizations, and public health agencies. They advise clients on such administrative matters as staff organization, nursing techniques, curricula, and education programs. Other administrative specialists include *educational directors for the state board of nursing*, who are concerned with maintaining well-defined educational standards, and *executive directors of professional nurses' associations*, who administer programs developed by the board of directors and the members of the association.

Some nurses choose to enter the armed forces. All types of nurses, except private duty nurses, are represented in the military services. They provide skilled nursing care to active-duty and retired members of the armed forces and their families. In addition to basic nursing skills, *military nurses* are trained to provide care in various environments, including field hospitals, on-air evacuation flights, and onboard ships. Military nurses actively influence the development of health care through nursing research. Advances influenced by military nurses include the development of the artificial kidney (dialysis unit) and the concept of the intensive care unit.

REQUIREMENTS

High School

If you are interested in becoming a registered nurse, you should take high school mathematics and science courses, including biology, chemistry, and physics. Health courses will also be helpful. English and speech courses should not be neglected because you must be able to communicate well with patients.

Postsecondary Training

There are three basic kinds of training programs that you may choose from to become a registered nurse: associate's degree, diploma, and bachelor's degree. Which of the three training programs to choose depends on your career goals. A bachelor's degree in nursing is required for most supervisory or administrative positions, for jobs in public health agencies, and for admission to graduate nursing programs. A master's degree is usually necessary to prepare for a nursing specialty or to teach. For some specialties, such as nursing research, a Ph.D. is essential.

There are more than 700 bachelor's degree programs in nursing in the United States. It requires four (in some cases, five) years to complete. The graduate of this program receives a bachelor of science in nursing (BSN) degree. The associate degree in nursing (ADN) is awarded after completion of a two-year study program that is usually offered in a junior or community college. There are approximately 700 ADN programs in the United States. You receive hospital training at cooperating hospitals in the general vicinity of the community college. The diploma program, which usually lasts three years, is conducted by hospitals and independent schools, although the number of these programs is declining. At the conclusion of each of these programs, you become a graduate nurse, but not, however, a registered nurse. To obtain the RN designation you must pass a licensing examination required in all states.

Nurses can pursue postgraduate training that allows them to specialize in certain areas, such as emergency room, operating room, premature nursery, or psychiatric nursing. This training is sometimes offered through hospital on-the-job training programs.

Certification or Licensing

Voluntary certification is available for a variety of registered nursing specialties, and certification may be required for the four advanced practice nursing specialties. Contact professional nursing associations in your specialty for more information on certification.

All states and the District of Columbia require a license to practice nursing. To obtain a license, graduates of approved nursing schools must pass a national examination, known as the National Council Licensure Examination. Nurses may be licensed by more than one state. In some states, continuing education is a condition for license renewal. Different titles require different education and training levels.

Other Requirements

You should enjoy helping people, especially those who may experience fear or anger because of an illness. Patience, compassion, and calmness are qualities needed by anyone working in this career. In addition, you must be able to give directions as well as follow instructions and work as part of a health care team. Anyone interested in becoming a registered nurse should also have a strong desire to continue learning because new tests, procedures, and technologies are constantly being developed for the medical world.

EXPLORING

You can explore your interest in nursing in a number of ways. Read books on careers in nursing and talk with high school counselors, school nurses, and local public health nurses. Visit hospitals to observe the work and talk with hospital personnel to learn more about the daily activities of nursing staff.

Some hospitals now have extensive volunteer service programs in which high school students may work after school, on weekends, or during vacations in order to both render a valuable service and to explore their interests. There are other volunteer work experiences available with the Red Cross or community health services. Camp counseling jobs sometimes offer related experiences. Some schools offer participation in Future Nurses programs.

The Internet is full of resources about nursing. Check out Nursing Net (http://www.nursingnet.org), Discover Nursing (http://www.discovernursing.com), and the American Nurses Association's Nursing World (http://www.nursingworld.org).

EMPLOYERS

Approximately 2.6 million RNs are employed in the United States. Inpatient and outpatient hospital departments account for about 3 out of 5 jobs for registered nurses. Nurses are employed by hospitals, managed care facilities, long-term care facilities, clinics, industry, private homes, schools, camps, and government agencies. One out of five nurses works part time.

STARTING OUT

The only way to become a RN is through completion of one of the three kinds of educational programs, plus passing the licensing examination. RNs may apply for employment directly to hospitals, nursing homes, home care agencies, temporary nursing agencies, companies, and government agencies that hire nurses. Jobs can also be obtained through school career services offices, by signing up with employment agencies specializing in placement of nursing personnel, or through the state employment office. Other sources of jobs include nurses' associations, professional journals, and newspaper want ads.

ADVANCEMENT

Increasingly, administrative and supervisory positions in the nursing field go to nurses who have earned at least the bachelor of science degree in nursing. Nurses with many years of experience who are graduates of a diploma program may achieve supervisory positions, but requirements for such promotions have become more difficult in recent years and in many cases require at least the BSN degree.

Nurses with bachelor's degrees are usually those who are hired as public health nurses. Nurses with master's degrees are often employed as faculty, instructors, supervisors, or administrators.

RNs can pursue further education to become advanced practice nurses, who have greater responsibilities and command higher salaries.

EARNINGS

According to the U.S. Department of Labor (DOL), RNs had median annual earnings of $63,750 in 2009. Salaries ranged from less than $43,970 to more than $93,700. Earnings of RNs vary according to employer. According to the DOL, those who worked at hospitals earned mean annual salaries of $67,740; those working in home health care services earned $63,300; and RNs who worked at nursing care facilities earned $59,320.

Salary is determined by several factors: setting, education, and work experience. Most full-time nurses are given flexible work schedules as well as health and life insurance; some are offered education reimbursement and year-end bonuses. A staff nurse's salary is limited only by the amount of work he or she is willing to take on. Many nurses take advantage of overtime work and shift differentials. About 10 percent of all nurses hold more than one job.

WORK ENVIRONMENT

Most nurses work in facilities that are clean and well lighted and where the temperature is controlled, although some work in run-down inner city hospitals in less-than-ideal conditions. Usually, nurses work eight-hour shifts. Those in hospitals generally work any of three shifts: 7:00 A.M. to 3:00 P.M.; 3:00 P.M. to 11:00 P.M.; or 11:00 P.M. to 7:00 A.M.

Nurses spend much of the day on their feet, either walking or standing. Handling patients who are ill or infirm can also be very exhausting. Nurses who come in contact with patients with infectious diseases must be especially careful about cleanliness and sterility. Although many nursing duties are routine, many responsibilities are unpredictable. Sick persons are often very demanding, or they may be depressed or irritable. Despite this, nurses must maintain their composure and should be cheerful to help the patient achieve emotional balance.

Community health nurses may be required to visit homes that are in poor condition or very dirty. They may also come in contact with social problems, such as family violence. The nurse is an important health care provider and in many communities the sole provider.

Both the office nurse and the industrial nurse work regular business hours and are seldom required to work overtime. In some jobs, such as where nurses are on duty in private homes, they may frequently travel from home to home and work with various cases.

OUTLOOK

The nursing field is the largest of all health care occupations, and employment prospects for nurses are excellent. The DOL projects that employment for registered nurses will grow much faster than the average for all professions through 2018. Opportunities will be strongest in the following sectors: offices of physicians and home health care services, where employment is expected to increase by 48 percent and 33 percent, respectively, through 2018; nursing care facilities, 25 percent; and employment services, 24 percent.

There has been a serious shortage of nurses in recent years. Many nurses leave the profession within five years because of unsatisfactory working conditions, including severe understaffing, high stress, physical demands, mandatory overtime, and irregular hours. The shortage will also be exacerbated by the increasing numbers of baby boomer aged nurses who are expected to retire, creating more open positions than there are graduates of nursing programs.

The strong growth in this field is also a result of improving medical technology that will allow for treatments of many more diseases and health conditions. Nurses will be in strong demand to work with the rapidly growing population of senior citizens in the United States.

Approximately 60 percent of all nursing jobs are found in hospitals. However, because of administrative cost cutting, increased nurses' workload, and rapid growth of outpatient services (such as those that provide same-day surgery, chemotherapy, and rehabilitation), hospital nursing jobs will experience slower growth as compared to other settings within the nursing profession. Despite this prediction, there should continue to be a need for RNs in critical care units, emergency departments, and operating rooms. These settings, which often are stressful and involve overtime and night and weekend shifts, frequently have shortages of RNs.

Employment in home care and nursing homes is expected to grow rapidly. Though more people are living well into their 80s and 90s, many need the kind of long-term care available at a nursing home. Also, because of financial reasons, patients are being released from hospitals sooner and admitted into nursing homes. Many nursing homes have facilities and staff capable of caring for long-term rehabilitation patients, as well as those afflicted with Alzheimer's. Many nurses will also be needed to help staff the growing number of outpatient facilities, such as HMOs, group medical practices, and ambulatory surgery centers.

RNs with a bachelor's degree or higher—especially those who work as advanced practice nurses—will have the strongest employment prospects.

Nursing specialties will be in great demand. There are, in addition, many part-time employment possibilities, with about 21 percent of RNs working part time.

FOR MORE INFORMATION

Visit the AACN Web site to access a list of member schools and to read the online pamphlet Your Nursing Career: A Look at the Facts.
American Association of Colleges of Nursing (AACN)
One Dupont Circle, NW, Suite 530
Washington, DC 20036-1135
Tel: 202-463-6930
http://www.aacn.nche.edu

For information about opportunities as an RN, contact the following organizations:
American Nurses Association
8515 Georgia Avenue, Suite 400
Silver Spring, MD 20910-3492
Tel: 800-274-4262
http://www.nursingworld.org

American Society of Registered Nurses
1001 Bridgeway, Suite 233
Sausalito, CA 94965-2104
Tel: 415-331-2700
E-mail: office@asrn.org
http://www.asrn.org

For information on certification, contact
American Nurses Credentialing Center
8515 Georgia Avenue, Suite 400
Silver Spring, MD 20910-3492
Tel: 800-284-2378
http://www.nursecredentialing.org

For information on licensing, contact
National Council of State Boards of Nursing
111 East Wacker Drive, Suite 2900
Chicago, IL 60601-4277
Tel: 312-525-3600
E-mail: info@ncsbn.org
https://www.ncsbn.org

For information about state-approved programs and information on nursing, contact the following organizations:
National League for Nursing
61 Broadway. 33rd Floor
New York, NY 10006-2701
Tel: 212-363-5555
E-mail: generalinfo@nln.org
http://www.nln.org

National Organization for Associate Degree Nursing
7794 Grow Drive
Pensacola, FL 32514-7072
Tel: 850-484-6948
E-mail: noadn@dancyamc.com
https://www.noadn.org

Discover Nursing, sponsored by Johnson & Johnson Services Inc., provides information on nursing careers, nursing schools, and scholarships.
Discover Nursing
http://www.discovernursing.com

School Nurses

OVERVIEW

School nurses focus on students' overall health. They may work in one school or in several, visiting each for a part of the day or week. They may also assist the school physician, if the school employs one. They work with parents, teachers, and other school and professional personnel to meet students' health needs. School nurses promote health and safety, work to prevent illnesses, treat accidents and minor injuries, maintain students' health records, and refer students who may need additional medical attention. School nurses may also be responsible for health education programs and school health plans. They are also in charge of administering medication to children and for seeing that special needs students' health requirements are met. School nurses are employed at the elementary, middle, and high school levels, as well as at colleges and universities.

HISTORY

The first school health services in the United States were provided in Boston public schools in 1894. School medical professionals examined students to ensure that they did not have communicable diseases such as scarlet fever, chicken pox, or measles. As a result of their work, the spread of these and other diseases was reduced and the number of absentee students declined.

The National Association of School Nurses cites 1902 as the founding of school nursing as we know it today. On October 1 of that year, a registered nurse named Lina Rogers Struthers was placed as an "experiment" in a New York City public school to help identify and reduce communicable diseases in students and promote good health. Her introduction was a great success, and school nurses were hired at other New York schools and those around the country. As more school nurses were hired, the association reports that their role expanded to "include an emphasis on student wellness, disease prevention and health education, not only for the student, but for family members and the community as well." Today, school nurses play a key role in schools at all educational levels.

THE JOB

"Many people think school nursing is simply putting bandages on skinned knees, but it is much more than that," says Sue Schilb, RN, a school nurse at an elementary school in Iowa for five years. "Of course, we take care of injured and sick children, but what most people don't realize is the amount of paperwork, planning, and record keeping that is involved in the job."

Schilb adds, "We must assess every child entering kindergarten and make sure the child has had all the required immunizations. In addition, we must maintain records on all the students, including state-mandated immunizations. We take the height and weight of each student every year, check their vision, and work with an audiologist to conduct hearing tests."

In addition to all the record-keeping tasks, school nurses are frequently a resource for parents or staff members. "We often interact with parents when their children are ill or if they have questions about their child's health," says Schilb. "If special needs children attend our school, we must develop a care plan for them to make sure their needs are met."

School nurses are also health educators. Teachers may ask the school nurse to speak to their individual classes when they are covering subjects that deal with health or safety. School nurses may also be required to make presentations such as disease prevention, health education, and environmental health and safety to the student body, staff, and parent organizations.

School nurses may be employed on a full- or part-time basis depending on the school's needs, their funding, their size, and their state's or district's requirements. Some school nurses may also be employed in private or parochial schools.

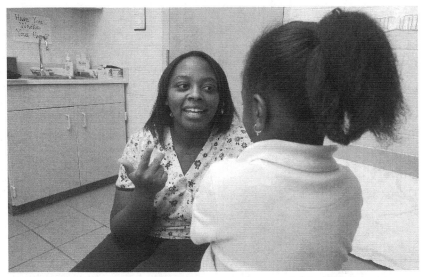

An elementary school nurse talks with a student about the importance of proper nutrition and exercise. *(Mickey Welsh,* Montgomery Advertiser/ *AP Photo)*

REQUIREMENTS

High School

Take as many science (especially biology and human anatomy), mathematics, psychology, computer science, and health classes as you can in high school. Other recommended courses include computer science, English, and speech.

Postsecondary Training

State requirements for school nurses vary. Some states have a certification requirement. Others require that their school nurses have bachelor's degrees while some do not require a bachelor's degree but do have specific educational requirements. There are some states that require their school nurses to be registered nurses.

There is no special program for school nursing; however, most nursing programs have courses geared to the specialty such as health education, child or adolescent psychology, crisis intervention, community health, and growth and development.

Many school nurses are graduates of practical nursing programs, which involve about one year of classroom instruction and supervised clinical practice, which usually takes place in a hospital.

There are three basic kinds of training programs that you may choose from to become a registered nurse: associate's degree, diploma, and bachelor's degree. Which of the three training programs to choose depends on your career goals. A bachelor's degree in nursing is the most popular method, however, as such a degree is required for most supervisory or administrative positions, for jobs in public health agencies, and for admission to graduate nursing programs. Diplomas are offered by three-year programs at schools of nursing and hospitals, and an associate's degree is obtained from a two-year college.

Certification or Licensing

Both licensed practical nurses and registered nurses must pass an examination after they have completed a state-approved nursing program. This is required by all states and the District of Columbia.

National certification is available through the National Board for Certification of School Nurses. Contact the board for information on certification requirements. Some states have certification requirements for school nurses; others offer voluntary certification programs. Check with your state's department of professional regulation for information on requirements in your state.

In addition, some state education agencies set requirements such as nursing experience and competency in specified areas of health and education. Local or regional boards of education may also have certain qualifications that they require of their school nurses.

Other Requirements

School nurses must have patience and like working with children and teens. They must also be able to work well with teachers, parents, administrators, and other health personnel. School nurses should be able to work independently since they often work alone.

EXPLORING

This is one area of nursing where you don't have far to travel to talk to someone in the career; of course, you should visit your own school nurse. Ask about his or her daily responsibilities and workload and how he or she prepared for this line of work. Ask for suggestions on nursing programs and other tips on starting your career.

See if your school or local institution offers first-aid programs to learn some basic emergency medical procedures such as CPR. Another way to gain experience is through volunteer work at a hospital, nursing home, or other medical facility.

EMPLOYERS

School nurses are employed by private and public schools at the elementary, middle, and high school levels, as well as at colleges and universities. The National Association of School Nurses reports that school nurses also work for departments of health, public health departments and agencies, hospitals, and hospital districts.

STARTING OUT

Many new nurses gain practical experience in a nonschool setting before they apply for employment as a school nurse. Nurses can apply directly to hospitals, nursing homes, and companies and government agencies that hire nurses. Jobs can also be obtained through school career services offices, by signing up with employment agencies specializing in placement of nursing personnel, or through the state employment office. Other sources of jobs include professional journals, newspaper want ads, and Internet job and social networking sites. Additionally, the National Association of School Nurses offers job listings at its Web site, http://www.nasn.org.

ADVANCEMENT

Administrative and supervisory positions in the nursing field go to nurses who have earned at least the bachelor of science degree in nursing (BSN). Nurses with many years of experience who are graduates of the diploma program may achieve supervisory positions, but requirements for such promotions have become more difficult in recent years and in many cases require at least the bachelor of science in nursing degree.

Some school nurses may advance to the position of *registered school nurse*. These professionals manage and oversee health aides employed in the schools. Others become *state school nurse consultants*, who help school districts and school nurses provide top-quality nursing services to students.

EARNINGS

School nurses' salaries are determined by several factors—the financial status of the school district, the nurse's experience, and the scope of duties. According to the U.S. Department of Labor (DOL), registered nurses had median annual earnings of $63,750 in 2009. Salaries ranged from less than $43,970 to more than $93,700. Licensed practical nurses made a median salary of $39,820 in 2009. The lowest paid 10 percent made less than $28,890, and the highest paid 10 percent made more than $55,090.

Employers offer a variety of benefit packages, which can include any of the following: paid holidays, vacations, and sick days; personal days; medical, dental, and life insurance; profit-sharing plans; 401(k) plans; and retirement and pension plans.

WORK ENVIRONMENT

Schools are found in all communities, cities, and rural areas, and learning institutions can vary greatly. School nurses may work in an environment that is a state-of-the-art educational institution in an affluent community, or they may work in a rundown building in the inner city. By the same token, some school nurses may have up-to-date equipment and adequate resources, while others may find that they have restricted funds that inhibit their ability to do their jobs.

School nurses usually work days and may have some time off during the summer months when school is not in session.

The increase in school violence impacts the school nurses' working environment since it is evident that acts of violence can occur in any institution in any community. School nurses must be prepared to deal with the physical results of violence in their schools.

School nurses may come in contact with infectious diseases and are often exposed to illnesses and injuries. All nursing careers have some health and disease risks; however, adherence to health and safety guidelines greatly minimizes the chance of contracting infectious diseases such as hepatitis and AIDS.

OUTLOOK

Nursing specialties will be in great demand in the future. In fact, according to the DOL, employment for registered nurses will grow much faster than the average for all careers through 2018. However, according to the National Association of School Nurses, even though school enrollments are projected to increase, school nurse positions are being eliminated in a greater proportion than other positions within the educational system. As educational systems try to find ways to cut costs, professionals such as school nurses may be eliminated. Since cuts may vary by region and state, school nurses should be flexible and willing to relocate or to seek other nursing opportunities, if necessary.

FOR MORE INFORMATION

For information on nursing education and careers, contact
American Association of Colleges of Nursing
One Dupont Circle, NW, Suite 530
Washington, DC 20036-1135
Tel: 202-463-6930
http://www.aacn.nche.edu

For information on union membership for school nurses, contact
American Federation of Teachers
555 New Jersey Avenue, NW
Washington, DC 20001-2029
Tel: 202-879-4400
http://www.aft.org/yourwork/healthcare

Visit the association's Web site for more information on school nurse careers, certification, and membership for nursing students.
National Association of School Nurses
8484 Georgia Avenue, Suite 420
Silver Spring, MD 20910-5623
Tel: 240-821-1130
E-mail: nasn@nasn.org
http://www.nasn.org

For more information on the career of state school nurse consultant, contact
National Association of State School Nurse Consultants
7263 State Route 43
PO Box 708
Kent, OH 44240-0013
http://www.nassnc.org

For information on certification, contact
National Board for Certification of School Nurses
1350 Broadway, 17th Floor
New York, NY 10018-7702
Tel: 888-776-2481
E-mail: certification@nbcsn.com
http://www.nbcsn.com

Transplant Coordinators

OVERVIEW

Transplant coordinators are involved in practically every aspect of organ procurement (getting the organ from the donor) and transplantation. There are two types of transplant coordinators: *procurement coordinators* and *clinical coordinators*. Procurement coordinators help the families of organ donors deal with the death of a loved one as well as inform them of the organ donation process. Clinical coordinators educate recipients about how to prepare for an organ transplant and how to care for themselves after the transplant.

HISTORY

Scientists have been conducting research regarding human and animal organ transplantation since the 18th century. Greater research led to refinements in transplant technology, and in 1954, the first successful human kidney transplant was performed in Boston. The 1960s brought many successes in the field of organ transplants, including successful human liver and pancreas transplants. The first heart transplant was performed in 1967.

Despite these successes, many transplants eventually failed because of the body's immune system, which eventually rejected the new organ as a foreign object. Although drugs were designed in the 1960s to help the body accept transplanted organs, it wasn't until the early 1980s that a truly effective immunosuppressant drug, cyclosporin, was available. This drug substantially improved the success rate of transplant surgeries. More precise tissue typing or matching of donor and recipient tissues also helped increase the success rate.

Though successful organ transplants have increased, some transplants still fail over time despite modern drug treatments and closer tissue matching. Research in this area continues with the hope of increasing the rate of successful transplants.

THE JOB

Transplant coordinators are involved in practically every aspect of organ procurement (getting the organ from the donor) and transplantation. This may involve working with medical records, scheduling surgeries, educating potential organ recipients, and counseling donor families.

There are two types of transplant coordinators: procurement coordinators and clinical coordinators. Although procurement and clinical coordinators are actively involved in evaluating, planning, and maintaining records, an important part of their job is helping individuals and families. Procurement coordinators help the families of organ donors deal with the death of their loved one and inform them of the organ donation process.

Clinical coordinators educate recipients in how to best prepare for organ transplant and how to care for themselves after the transplant. Many coordinators, especially clinical coordinators, are registered nurses, but it is not necessary to have a nursing degree to work as a coordinator. Some medical background is important, however. Many transplant coordinators have degrees in biology, physiology, accounting, psychology, business administration, or public health.

Once the donor patient has been declared brain dead and is no longer breathing on his or her own, the procurement transplant coordinator approaches the donor's family about organ donation. If the family gives its consent, the coordinator then collects medical information and tissue samples for analysis. The coordinator also calls the United Network for Organ Sharing (UNOS), a member organization that includes every transplant program, organ procurement organization (OPO), and tissue-typing laboratory in the United States. The UNOS attempts to match organs with recipients within the OPO's region. If no local match can be made, the coordinator must make arrangements for the organs to be delivered to another state. In either case, the procurement coordinator schedules an operating room for the removal of the organs and coordinates the surgery.

Transplant Statistics, 2009

Total transplants: 28,463

Total number of donors: 14,624

Total number of female donors: 7,277 (3,294 deceased)

Total number of male donors: 7,347 (4,727 deceased)

Age group with the highest number of recipients: 50–64

Age group with the highest number of donors: 50–64

State with the highest number of transplants: California (3,058 transplants)

Source: United Network for Organ Sharing

Once the organs have been removed and transported, clinical transplant coordinators take over. Clinical transplant coordinators have been involved in preparing recipients for new organs. It is the clinical coordinators' job to see to the patients' needs before, during, and after organ transplants. This involves admitting patients, contacting surgeons, and arranging for operating rooms, as well as contacting the anesthesiology department and the blood bank. Transplant coordinators educate patients and arrange for blood tests and other tests to make sure patients can withstand the rigors of surgery. They help patients register on organ waiting lists. They make sure patients have a support system of family, friends, and caregivers in place. After the transplants, coordinators help patients through their recovery by helping them understand their medications, arranging for routine doctor visits and lab tests, and informing them about danger signs of organ rejection.

Another significant aspect of the job of all transplant coordinators is educating the public about the importance of organ donation. They speak to hospital and nursing school staffs and to the general public to encourage donations.

REQUIREMENTS

High School

High school courses that will prepare you for a medical-based education will be the most valuable in this profession. Science courses such as biology and chemistry are important, as are courses in psychology, sociology, math, and health.

If you live near a transplant center, there may be volunteer opportunities available at the center or in an outpatient care home for transplant recipients. Your local Red Cross also may need volunteers for promoting donor awareness.

Postsecondary Training
There is no specific educational track for transplant coordinators. One transplant coordinator may focus on financing and insurance, while another may work on education and awareness. Another coordinator may perform physical tests and evaluations, while another counsels grieving families. The more experience and education with health care and medicine you have, the better your job opportunities. Although a nursing degree isn't required of all coordinators, it does give you a good medical background. A bachelor's degree in one of the sciences, along with experience in a medical setting, will also open up job opportunities. Some people working as coordinators may have master's degrees in public health or in business administration. Other coordinators may hold doctorates in psychology or social work.

Certification or Licensing
Certification, though not required, is available through the American Board for Transplant Certification. To qualify for certification, you must have completed a year of full-time work as a coordinator.

There are four separate tests given—one for clinical transplant coordinators, one for procurement transplant coordinators, one for certified transplant preservationists, and one for certified clinical transplant nurses. The tests cover all organs and ask questions about analysis, treatment, and education of patients.

Other Requirements
To be a successful transplant coordinator, you should have good organizational skills and be able to work quickly, accurately, and efficiently. You must be a detail-oriented person and have good record-keeping and reporting skills. A transplant coordinator needs to be a compassionate person who is able to communicate well with doctors, patients, donors' families, and the public.

EXPLORING
To learn more about the work of transplant coordinator, research the organ transplant process as much as possible. The Internet and

your local library are great resources for information. A glossary of transplant-related terms is available at http://www.transplantliving .org/community/glossary.aspx. Another useful Web site is Transplant Experiences (http://www.transplantexperience.com), which provides an overview of the transplant process. Talk to your school counselor about your possible interest in health care. He or she may be able to suggest different programs to research or, better yet, give you names of previous students to talk to who have gone on to medical programs. Volunteering at local hospitals or health care clinics can give you experience working with patients.

Because much of a transplant coordinator's job involves communicating with patients and their family members during times of high stress, explore your interest and talent in counseling and social work in addition to medicine.

EMPLOYERS

A number of different institutions and organizations require transplant coordinators. In addition to transplant centers across the country, there are organ procurement organizations and tissue-typing labs. These organizations and centers may be hospital-based, independent, or university-based.

STARTING OUT

Positions for transplant coordinators are advertised nationally in medical publications and on the Internet. NATCO, The Organization for Transplant Professionals (http://www.natco1.org) and the International Transplant Nurses Society (http://www.itns.org) offer job listings at their Web sites.

Many transplant coordinators begin their professional careers in other areas such as nursing, business, psychology, social work, or the sciences before they seek a career as a transplant coordinator.

ADVANCEMENT

There may be internal advancement opportunities within a clinic such as senior coordinator or senior educator. Other managerial or supervisory positions may also be a way of advancing within the career. There are other aspects of transplantation, such as surgery or hospital administration, that may be available with additional education and experience.

EARNINGS

Salaries vary based on educational background, experience, and responsibilities of the coordinator. People who have a degree and work as directors or educators may earn a higher salary than those working at the clinical end. According to Payscale.com, annual salaries for transplant coordinators ranged from $57,964 to $95,000, with median earnings of $65,000 in 2010.

Many transplant coordinators are registered nurses. Salaries are comparable to those of registered nurses in other fields. Median annual earnings of registered nurses were $63,750 in 2009, according to the U.S. Department of Labor (DOL). Salaries ranged from less than $43,970 to more than $93,700. Some transplant coordinators are physician assistants, who had median annual earnings of $84,420 in 2009, according to the DOL, with salaries ranging from less than $55,880 to more than $115,080 a year.

Although transplant centers and organ procurement agencies are nonprofit organizations, transplant coordinators generally receive very good health and retirement benefits that are consistent with other medical professions.

WORK ENVIRONMENT

Transplant coordinators can be found doing their jobs in various environments. They may be in an office completing paperwork, in a hospital visiting with patients, families, or other hospital staff, in a clinic or doctor's office seeing patients, or at a school or business meeting promoting donor awareness. Sometimes coordinators must accompany the organ to the transplant center, and some may be required to be on call and to work long, irregular hours.

OUTLOOK

The number of people waiting for organ donations is increasing, but there still is a need to find an increased number of donors. Therefore, a number of organizations have been developed to promote organ donations, particularly among minorities. These efforts require the skills of transplant coordinators. Because the stress level of the job is high, the burnout rate is also high. Also, because procurement coordinators' hours can be long and irregular, many procurement coordinators move on to other positions after only 18 months or less. This means continued job opportunities for those looking for work as coordinators.

FOR MORE INFORMATION

The following organization provides information on a career as a transplant coordinator and the certification process:
American Board for Transplant Certification
PO Box 15384
Lenexa, KS 66285-5384
Tel: 913-895-4603
E-mail: abtc-info@goamp.com
http://www.abtc.net

The following organizations provide information on a career as a transplant coordinator:
International Transplant Nurses Society
1739 East Carson Street, Box 351
Pittsburgh, PA 15203-1700
Tel: 412-343-4867
E-mail: itns@msn.com
http://www.itns.org

NATCO, The Organization for Transplant Professionals
PO Box 15384
Lenexa, KS 66285-5384
Tel: 913-895-4612
E-mail: natco-info@goAMP.com
http://www.natco1.org

United Network for Organ Sharing
PO Box 2484
Richmond, VA 23218-2484
Tel: 804-782-4817
http://www.unos.org

Index